UPCYCLING CELEBRATIONS

A Use-What-You-Have Guide to Decorating, Gift-Giving & Entertaining

by Danny Seo

Photographs by Laura Moss

RUNNING PRESS
PHILADELPHIA · LONDON

© 2012 by Danny Seo Media Ventures
Published by Running Press,
A Member of the Perseus Books Group

All rights reserved under the Pan-American and International Copyright Conventions
Printed in China

Books published by Running Press are available at special discounts for bulk purchases in the United States by corporations, institutions, and other organizations. For more information, please contact the Special Markets Department at the Perseus Books Group, 2300 Chestnut Street, Suite 200, Philadelphia, PA 19103, or call (800) 810-4145, ext. 5000, or e-mail special.markets@perseusbooks.com.

ISBN 978-0-7624-4466-3
Library of Congress Control Number: 2012938584

E-book ISBN 978-0-7624-4709-1

9   8   7   6   5   4   3   2   1
Digit on the right indicates the number of this printing

Cover and Interior design by Jason Kayser
Interior Photographs by Laura Moss
Edited by Jennifer Kasius
Typography: Meta, Minion, and United

Running Press Book Publishers
2300 Chestnut Street
Philadelphia, PA 19103-4371

Visit us on the web!
www.runningpress.com

CONTENTS

I could not celebrate the success of
this book if it weren't for you, the readers, who
have understood and embraced the whole
upcycling philosophy. Thank you for picking up the
glue gun, going through your recycling bin,
and for upcycling away.

INTRODUCTION

I've thrown all sorts of parties over the years.

They've ranged from the casual get-togethers with friends in my home to over-the-top corporate events with hundreds of people on the guest list. They've been very grown-up affairs with truffled meals, formal letterpress invitations, and fragrant flowers, to the polar opposite of the spectrum with children bouncing in a giant inflatable castle with faces painted to resemble everything from butterflies to skull and cross bones. But if there's one thing all of these celebrations have in common, it is that anyone who comes to one of my parties is guaranteed to have a great time.

Stress-free entertaining is nothing new. No book can promise to help you be "stress-free" because really the root of anxiety comes from the host, not from the ideas. So, I want to emphasize this: Remember, nobody has a good time if the person in charge is an emotional basket case. You're having a party, not performing open-heart surgery.

Now that I've got that out of the way, I will promise you this: All of the projects in this celebrations book are easy, inexpensive, and use things we may already have, in unexpected and oh-so functional ways.

Unlike my previous book, *Upcycling,* which had loads of ideas to decorate your home with a smattering of gift-giving and entertaining ideas, this book is all parties, all the time.

As a host, event planner, and home cook, I've learned a lot of ideas along the way that I call my foolproof arsenal of party tricks. And as an upcycler who lives and breathes by the mantra of transforming trash into beautiful new things, I don't just write the books, but I live it, and this book is evidence of that.

A few rules I live by: a very famous fashion stylist with a popular reality show once told me they tell their clients to take off one piece of jewelry before they head out the door to an event; maybe earrings, a necklace, *and* a tiara is a bit too much. I like this rule a lot and I will look at my laundry list of things I want at a party and knock something off. Less is always more when it comes to the décor and activities. (But more is never less when it comes to the food and drink!)

Here's another tip: Don't do gift bags. Nobody wants personalized little tins of mints or a bottle of water with your parents' names on it and "35th Anniversary Bash!" But don't be a Scrooge and tell your friends and family "no gifts" when it comes to your own birthday; it robs them of the job of giving you something they think you'll really love. Just remember: That's why national retailers have liberal return policies.

Finally, try not to break the upcycling rule by using new materials instead of old. Of course it would be easier to go to the store and buy new straws, plastic utensils, and fabric than to rummage trash bins and thrift shops. But the point of upcycling is more than economical, it's also ecological. Keeping something out of our landfills gives the finished upcycled item more meaning than looking pretty; it's been given a second chance to be something even greater than it was originally meant to be.

CHAPTER ONE:
NEW YEAR'S CELEBRATIONS

I've been the go-to guy for my friends to be the host of almost every New Year's Eve party for the past ten years. I think it has to do with the fact that I live in Bucks County, Pennsylvania, way outside the hustle and bustle of New York City. I know what you're thinking: Isn't NYC where most people go to be near Times Square, all the great parties, the fun, and debauchery? Yes, they do and it's fabulous to do at least once in your life. But eventually you realize that being warm, with friends, well-fed and in bed at a certain hour is more appealing than drunkenly trying to find a cab ride home at three in the morning. So bucolic Bucks County wins!

One thing I've learned over the years is that New Year's is not to be confused with Halloween; people don't like dressing up or pretending they are in 1920s Prohibition era, so think twice about hosting a theme party. Instead, guests like being comfortable. Correction: They like the permission to be comfortable. So dress like you would normally do at home: think jeans and a T-shirt. I avoid the formal sit-down dinner; people like to pick at things and snack all night long. They also love easy access to a plethora of drinks (both alcoholic and non) and to be in a room where music is playing—maybe even a network countdown on TV in the background. I usually skip dessert altogether and find that a simple fire roaring in the fireplace with a selection of S'mores ingredients can make even the grouchiest guest put a smile on their face. If you don't have a fireplace, lots of candles will do to create some ambience. (Candles, however, aren't the best at melting S'Mores!)

Finally, keep the decorating to a minimum; think big with ceiling decorations, some streamers, and maybe a festive sign or two. Avoid the temptation to buy those throwaway hats, noisemakers, and funny glasses at the store; nobody will wear them anyway and you just end up tossing them into the trash the next day. An upcycling no-no!

PLASTIC BAG PARTY BALLS

SUPPLIES: HUNDREDS OF USED PLASTIC SHOPPING BAGS (IN WHATEVER COLOR YOU WANT) ⊕ CHINESE PAPER LANTERNS (FROM A PARTY-SUPPLY STORE) ⊕ SCISSORS ⊕ SCOTCH TAPE ⊕ HOT-GLUE GUN WITH GLUE STICKS.

I want to preface this project by saying this: Do not visit your local supermarket and swipe a pile of new plastic bags when the checkout clerk isn't looking. One: That would be illegal. And, two: That would defeat the purpose of upcycling.

Instead, when looking for a stash of used plastic bags, ask your friends and family if they can empty their drawers for you; or you could even post a request on Facebook. You'll be surprised how quickly you'll amass a large collection of bags to make these festive hanging party balls.

When making this project, you have the choice of either doing a solid color, stripes, or a kaleidoscope of colors. If you don't have enough plastic bags to cover a whole lantern, you can also do bands of plastic poufs around the middle or create something sporadic. You really can do whatever design you want.

HOW TO: To make a plastic bag pouf, start by laying two bags of identical size on top of each other. ⊕ Then roll the bags up into a long strip and fold them in half length-wise. ⊕ Then fold it again length-wise and add a piece of tape in the middle so it resembles a bow tie. ⊕ Then snip the ends about ½-inch in at each end. ⊕ Fluff into a plastic pouf. ⊕ Hot glue these poufs all over the outside of the Chinese paper lantern until the entire lantern is covered. Hang using string or clear filament.

LED LIGHT WINTERIZED BULBS

SUPPLIES: LIGHT-EMITTING DIODE (LED) LIGHT BULBS (THEY CAN BE FOUND AT ANY HOME-IMPROVEMENT STORE LIKE LOWE'S) ✚ SEA GLASS OR RECYCLED GLASS CHIPS FROM THE CRAFT STORE (THESE ARE FROM MICHAELS) ✚ HOT-GLUE GUN.

The future of lighting is here and it's called LED, or Light-emitting diodes. If you've never heard of these bulbs, you definitely interact with them every day: traffic lights, most flat-screen televisions, and the clear glow of every BlackBerry and iPhone uses LED technology to light up. In the past, household LED bulbs used to be very expensive, but recently have become more affordable. And they are gaining popularity, too: The bulbs are super energy-efficient, last an incredibly long time (up to 25 years), and do not get hot to the touch, so they are safe. And light bulbs that stay cool also mean they are perfect to adorn with translucent glass crystals.

What I love about this upcycling idea is that the glowing bulbs look like they've been encrusted with icicles. For your New Year's party, unscrew a few LED bulbs from light fixtures and screw them into single-socket light cord (I got this from IKEA; it's called a Hemma cord set) as shown here. Group a bunch together and hang them from the ceiling all lit up. When the party is over, the cooled hot glue peels right off, leaving you with a clean bulb you can reuse for your lighting fixtures.

HOW TO: Pick through the bag of recycled glass chunks or sea glass and look for the nicest pieces that have a flat surface that will sit flush against the bottom of the bulb. ✚ Use hot glue to attach to the LED bulb and keep adding glass until you achieve the desired look.

PERSONALITY BUD VASES

SUPPLIES: EMPTY GLASS BOTTLES ✪ SCULPEY BRAND OVEN-BAKE CLAY ✪ VALSPAR BRILLIANT METAL SPRAY PAINT (AT LOWE'S STORES).

In my previous book, *Upcycling*, one of the rules I followed for all the projects was that they all had to be accomplished in three steps or less. Yes, sometimes one step would be more time-consuming or complicated than the other, but it was usually always three steps. In the case of this project, it is still three steps, but the end result will look like you've spent hours and not minutes making this.

This is a fun project to do with the kids; they can wash and dry the bottle, sculpt the faces of their characters with their hands and the parents can coat the finished bottle with a few coats of shimmery spray paint. Your personality bottles can be joyful, smug, serious or outright mean; but most importantly, be sure you have fun making them.

HOW TO: Rummage through your recycling bin for interesting-shaped glass bottles; I used Orangina for the smaller ones and an apple juice container for the larger one shown in the photo. ✪ Wash them well and thoroughly dry them. ✪ Use pieces of Sculpey bake-able clay (any color will do since it will be painted: available at Michaels craft stores) and use your fingers to mold eyes, a nose, lips, hair, and anything else you want to give your bottles personality. ✪ Press the clay pieces firmly onto the glass. ✪ Place them on top of the metal baking rack inside the oven. ✪ Bake them in the oven at 275°F for about 15 minutes until the polymer clay has set. ✪ When cool, spray a few light coats of spray paint and display.

It seems to happen at most (fun) parties: Many guests overindulge in rich food and alcoholic drinks. To help your guests ring in the New Year without too much regret, upcycle empty Altoid mint tins into mini SOS gift tins. Fill them with the get-well essentials they might need: aspirin for headaches, antacids for a stomachache, eye drops for dry eyes, and vitamins to revitalize the mind, body, and soul the next day. Giving these out at the beginning of a party could even help guests think twice about overindulging.

SOS ALTOID RESCUE TINS

SUPPLIES: EMPTY ALTOID TINS ✦ TRAVEL-SIZE PACKETS OF ASPIRIN, EYE DROPS, VITAMINS, AND ANY OTHER OVER-THE-COUNTER HANGOVER CURES ✦ SPARE CASH FOR CAB FARE ✦ CRAFT GLUE ✦ BRUSH ✦ BAND-AIDS AND DECORATIVE PAPER TO COVER THE TINS.

HOW TO: To cover the tins, simply cut strips of decorative paper to size to cover the top, bottom, and sides of the tins and adhere it with a light coat of white craft glue. ✦ Decorate with a Band-Aid that you can hand-stamp "SOS" on top for fun and fill with all the get-well essentials.

Forget the lampshades. On New Year's Eve, all of your guests will likely end up wearing a bejeweled candy crown at some point in the festive evening. Even though I talked about abstaining from party hats at the beginning of the chapter, here's one regal crown that may be useful to have on hand just in case things border between civil and silly. You can even recycle these to use at birthday parties to crown the guest of honor.

CANDY CROWN

SUPPLIES: SUGAR-FREE CANDIES ❖ HOT-GLUE GUN ❖ SCISSORS ❖ CEREAL BOX.

HOW TO: Flatten a cereal box and use a pencil to sketch out the shape of a crown, keeping in mind that the more basic and exaggerated the silhouette, the better. ❖ Cut it out with scissors and use hot glue to attach to two end pieces of the crown together so it becomes a crown that fits comfortably around the head. ❖ Then use hot glue to attach candies all over the crown. Sugar-free candies work best because they adhere better using glue and are less sticky to the touch.

I can't imagine being at a New Year's Eve party that is super brightly lit like a hospital waiting room. One of the best ways to cast a festive mood is to incorporate all sorts of mood lighting at your party: tealights in colored glass votives scattered throughout, dimmers on overhead pendant lights, fire from a roaring fireplace, and accent lighting from these illuminated balls.

As I mentioned earlier, LED technology also means the bulbs do not get hot to the touch, so it is super important that you only create this project using LED lights and not traditional strings of holiday lights, which do get hot and can be a fire hazard.

MINI TIMES-SQUARE LIGHT BALLS

SUPPLIES: LED STRING LIGHTS.

HOW TO: To make them couldn't be easier: Just wrap them onto themselves to make a ball; for larger sizes, connect multiple strands and keep wrapping. ✚ Plug them in and either hang from the ceiling, display in baskets, inside a non-working fireplace, or just scatter here and there for a little festive glow.

Thrift stores like Goodwill and Salvation Army are great places to find inexpensive picture frames in all sorts of styles and sizes, so this can be a very affordable upcycling project if you shop right. One fun way to invite a small group of people to your home is to send out a glittery New Year's invitation in a frame. Or you can make a few and scatter them throughout—on the counter in the bathroom, one by the bar, maybe one on the buffet table—to decorate with a little festive flair. They don't have to proclaim Happy New Year's; if your party is a little more formal, you can also use them to identify all the delicious items on your buffet.

GLITTERY NEW YEAR'S FRAMES

SUPPLIES: PICTURE FRAMES WITH GLASS FRONTS ⊙ CHUNKY GLITTER ⊙ HEAVY CARDSTOCK PAPER ⊙ SCISSORS OR CUTTING BOARD ⊙ AN ALPHABET STAMP SET AND INKPAD ⊙ BLACK ELECTRICAL TAPE.

HOW TO: First, mismatched frames can be unified by painting them all one color; choose whatever works best for your décor. ⊙ Pop out the back of the frame and use it as a template for your cardstock. ⊙ Trace the frame and cut it out with scissors or a cutting board. ⊙ Stamp the cardstock with whatever message you like. ⊙ Sprinkle glitter inside the frame on top of the glass, place the cardstock on top, and attach the original backing to the frame. ⊙ Shake the frame to scatter the glitter inside. If the backing isn't secure enough and glitter falls out, you can also tape the edges with black electrical tape on the back to create a secure closure.

I have no idea what a roll of real aluminum duct tape is actually for other than the fact it's one fantastical tape to unravel and stick all over branches to turn them from boring wood into high-tech metallic.

METALLIC ALUMINUM BRANCHES

SUPPLIES: BRANCHES FROM THE YARD ✪ REAL ALUMINUM DUCT TAPE (HYDROFORM BRAND AT THE HARDWARE STORE) ✪ TALL GLASS VASE ✪ WIDE GROSGRAIN RIBBON ✪ ARTIFICIAL BIRDS (FROM THE CRAFT STORE) ✪ VALSPAR METALLIC SPRAY PAINT (WE USED SILVER) ✪ FLORIST WIRE (OPTIONAL) ✪ ALPHABET STAMP SET AND INKPAD.

HOW TO: Simply unravel a section of aluminum tape, remove the waxy backing, and stick it on the branches; use your fingers to meld it into every little nook and cranny on the branch. The übersticky tape will adhere easily. If it tears or buckles in certain areas, just repair it with smaller piece of tape and burnish it with your fingers. I promise you: It is absolutely foolproof to work with this tape. ✪ Do several branches and display your High-Tech Mother Nature bouquet in a tall glass vase. ✪ Decorate with spray-painted silver birds and attach with florist wire. Or upcycle a piece of grosgrain ribbon and hand-stamp a festive message.

I have a complicated relationship with confetti. I think it's great if I'm in a public setting like Times Square where millions of pieces of confetti flitter down and create a party-like atmosphere. But I hate it if people are tossing it in the air in my home and leaving me with the household chore of cleaning it all up the next day. Not exactly the way I want to spend my New Year's Day, vacuuming up the mess.

But this book is not my platform to rant about the drudgery of cleaning, so if you do want to make upcycled confetti, here's my rather simple way to do it. Just don't expect to find any to toss at my party.

HOMEMADE CONFETTI

SUPPLIES: ALUMINUM FOIL ✪ COLORFUL SCRAP OR OFFICE PAPER ✪ OLD BLENDER.

HOW TO: If at all possible, use an old blender that still works but you have stashed away and have no intention of ever making a fresh-fruit smoothie in ever again. ✪ If you don't have an old blender, visit your local Goodwill store and try to find one for a song. ✪ With the lid on top, turn on the blender and toss in bits of paper, a little aluminum foil for shine and keep adding so it shreds almost instantly when it hits the blades. ✪ Do this in small batches and empty the confetti into a bowl as you go along until you have enough for your party.

It may seem to many of you that I do not know what candy is: I've used mints to make glittery crowns, and threaded gumdrops for garlands in trees seen in the pages of *Country Home* magazine. I've done everything but actually *eat* the candy. But here's an upcycling project an upcycler with a sweet tooth can love: a sweet necklace you can wear and then enjoy after the party.

GUMBALL COUTURE

SUPPLIES: GUMBALLS IN DIFFERENT SIZES AND COLORS ✪ SKINNY RIBBON OR SILK CORD ✪ CORDLESS DRILL WITH BITS.

HOW TO: Use a $\frac{5}{32}$-inch drill bit to drill a hole through each gumball. ✪ Use medium- to large-size gumballs (found at specialty candy stores) and not the regular-size ones since they tend to break and are difficult to drill. ✪ Thread your ribbon or cord through the hole and tie a knot.

I don't know if this is really a New Year's Eve idea or not, but antlers always conjure images of upstate cabins in the middle of winter, so here it is.

No matter what side of the animal-righteous fence you sit on when it comes to displaying mounted deer antlers, both vegans and outdoorsmen can feel good about this project. All you need are some gnarly or interesting branches that you collect on a walk through the woods. Look for fresh branches still on trees and not those fallen on the ground; they'll mount better and dry without the chance of rot when you hang them indoors.

"BRANCHLERS"

SUPPLIES: BRANCHES FROM THE YARD ✪ UNFINISHED WOODEN PLAQUES (IN THE UNPAINTED-WOOD CRAFTS SECTION AT THE CRAFT STORE) ✪ WOOD SCREWS ✪ CORDLESS DRILL ✪ PAINT (I USED VALSPAR GOLD BRILLIANT METALLICS SPRAY PAINT).

HOW TO: Paint unfinished wooden plaques any color of your choice and allow to dry. Look for branches that mimic the look of deer antlers. ✪ Drill a wood screw from behind the plaque and into the cut end of the branches; repeat to create the look of antlers. ✪ Mount on the wall.

CLOCKWISE FROM TOP LEFT:
CHAMPAGNE CHILLER, WINE CORK FIRE-STARTERS,
MAGNETIC TABS

CHAMPAGNE CHILLER, WINE CORK FIRE-STARTERS, AND MAGNETIC TABS

One of the fun things about a New Year's party is that even though you may want to be "grown-up" about it with your choice of dishes, music, and décor, it's still supposed to be a festive event to ring in the New Year. Here's a fun but practical way to keep all those bottles of champers icy cold: upcycle your gel beauty masks into bottle chillers. Simply freeze the masks and attach them to the bottles. They'll keep them cold and give those bottles of bubbly a little personality, too.

And once the wine and champagne have been drunk, upcycle those corks into useful fire-starters. It couldn't be any simpler: Fill a glass jar with genuine wine corks (no plastic ones!) as packed as possible and pour 91 percent isopropyl rubbing alcohol until it reaches the top of the jar. Screw on the lid and allow to soak. In just a few hours, the corks will be fully saturated and you can pull one out and light it to start a fire in the fireplace or save them for a summertime backyard grill. Keep the corks in a tightly sealed container and use them throughout the year.

Finally, the metal tabs on top of the champagne cage can be upcycled into useful and elegant magnets for your refrigerator or office. Simply pop them out of the metal cage and hot glue a magnet on the back.

CHAPTER TWO:
VALENTINE'S DAY

If you're single, Valentine's Day is a totally made-up holiday by corporations who are greedy to get every dollar from you in the form of flowers, chocolates, and paper cards. If you're in a relationship, Valentine's Day is the most romantic time of the year.

So, it's safe to say that V-Day can also be more than a lovey-dovey day for your sweetie. Whether it's to give a gift to a friend, family member, or to make homemade Valentine's Day with your children, February 14 doesn't have to only be a commercialized holiday, but it can also be a day to celebrate your loved ones.

This chapter has lots of ideas for both kids and adults, but they all have a grown-up aesthetic sensibility. Choose a few that look fun to you and make some lovely upcycled creations.

ROCK GRAVEL CHARM NECKLACES

SUPPLIES: SMALL RIVER ROCKS OR DRIVEWAY GRAVEL ✚ WHITE CRAFT PAINT ✚ FINE-TIP BRUSH ✚ E-6000 GLUE ✚ BEAD END CAP (AVAILABLE IN THE JEWELRY CRAFTING AISLE OR FIREMOUNTAINGEMS.COM) ✚ RED TWINE.

When I had a truckload of crushed-stone driveway gravel delivered to my house, I looked through handfuls of rocks, searching for the perfect heart-shaped stone. My thought was simple: a perfect upcycling project for Valentine's Day could involve a little hunting for Mother Nature's heart-designed rock that could be made into a simple, yet striking, charm necklace. Well, a few hours later I had rock rage, so I tweaked it a bit and like this result much better. This project can be done by a child or elevated into a beautiful piece of jewelry by someone with a very steady hand with the paintbrush.

HOW TO: Start off by collecting interesting pebbles and stones that fit flush inside the bead end cap; drop a little E-6000 glue inside the cap and press it onto the rock. ✚ Allow to dry completely. Use white craft paint and a fine-tip brush to adorn the rock with whatever message or design you want. ✚ Run a piece of red twine or silk cord through the loop on top of the cap holder.

I'm absolutely fascinated by the numerous types of spray paints in the market and the different finishes you can do with them. Traditional spray paint applied to plastic can create uneven and cracked finishes, so it's particularly important to use a paint designed for plastic for this project. While you can choose whatever color you want, I think red bottles declaring your LOVE for someone has the best result here. If you do decide to toss the bottles away after you've upcycled them, just remember this: They now can't be recycled because of the paint. So think about maybe saving them for the next time you feel a little bit in love.

PLASTIC LOVE BOTTLES

SUPPLIES: CLEAR PLASTIC BOTTLES ✪ RED PLASTIC SPRAY PAINT ✪ DUCT-TAPE STICKER SHEETS (AVAILABLE FROM MICHAELS CRAFT STORES) ✪ SCISSORS.

HOW TO: Cut out a set of letters for "O" and "V" using the duct-tape sheet; cut out one sticker for "L" and "E" and then flip the duct-tape sheet and cut out another set of "L" and "E" stickers so you have a mirror-image pair. ✪ Peel each letter and place one letter on the front of the bottle and another one on the back in the same place so it appears they are perfectly lined up; after you paint the bottles and peel off the stickers, it will appear like a "window" so you can read the letters clearly. ✪ In a well-ventilated area, spray it with two light coats of paint and allow to dry. ✪ Remove the stickers and fill with water and arrange flowers.

GLITTERED GRAPE VINES

SUPPLIES: GRAPE STEMS ✦ SPRAY ADHESIVE ✦ GLITTER ✦ SMALL GLASS BOTTLES OR BOWL ✦ PAPER (OPTIONAL) ✦ SCISSORS (OPTIONAL).

I think the No. 1 question I get from people is where on earth do I get my ideas and inspiration for the projects. I get them from all sorts of places, but really they come from my everyday interactions with trash and a wandering mind. Case in point: I was eating a snack-pack of cheese and grapes at my local Starbucks one morning and kept staring at the discarded grape stem sitting in front of me. It looked like a little dead tree to me. I brought it home and let it dry out on the kitchen counter and thought with a little glue and glitter, stems could become charming coral-like arrangements.

HOW TO: Save grape stems when you eat them and pick off any residual flesh or skin from grapes that weren't fully plucked off. ✦ Dry them off with a paper towel and allow them to dry for a few days. ✦ When you're ready to glitter, spray a light coat of spray adhesive all over the stem and sprinkle with glitter (red seems to work best, but use whatever color you want). ✦ Arrange in small glass bottles or place a cluster inside a bowl. ✦ Add hand-cut paper hearts to adorn if you desire.

Someone once said to me, "You must just sit at home and spend hours and hours crafting away when you have free time!" I hated to destroy her illusions, but I am the world's laziest crafter: I want to spend the least amount of time on a project and still get the maximum result. For my fellow lethargic crafters, this upcycling project is for you. Or, if you simply forgot to get a dozen roses on Valentine's Day, here's a handmade bouquet you can make yourself in minutes.

STYROFOAM HEARTS

SUPPLIES: STYROFOAM PACKAGING (WE SAVED THIS FROM THE PROTECTIVE PACKAGING INSIDE A CARTON HOLDING A TELEVISION) ✪ HEART-SHAPED COOKIE CUTTER ✪ BRANCHES FROM THE YARD.

HOW TO: Start off by finding a sharp, durable, well-made heart-shaped cookie cutter. If you can squeeze it very easily, it will literally break your heart when you attempt this project, so go with quality on this one. Simply press the cookie cutter into the Styrofoam packaging, and push it all the way through until the entire inside of the cutter is full of foam. ✪ Use your fingers to gently nudge it out; stick on top of a branch and arrange.

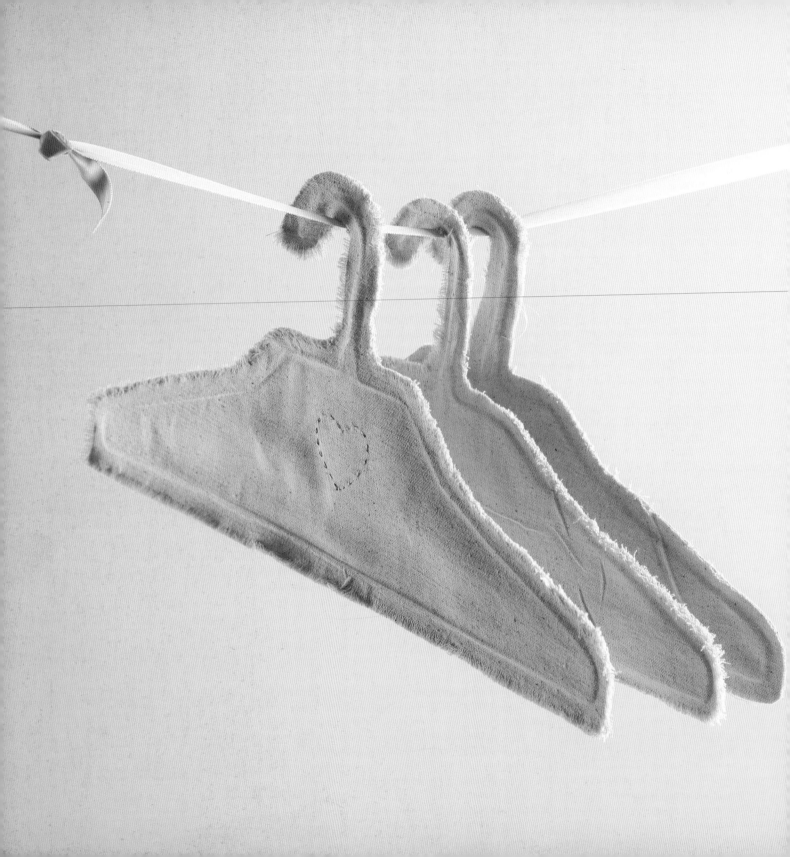

FABRIC-COVERED DRY-CLEANER HANGERS

SUPPLIES: WIRE DRY-CLEANER HANGERS ✚ COTTON PAINTER'S TARP ✚ LIQUID STITCH FABRIC GLUE ✚ SCISSORS.

I once brought my set of wooden hangers to the dry cleaner in the hopes they'd use them instead of the flimsy wire ones they usually use. When I came back to pick up my clothes, my sweaters and jackets were there, the hangers were not. While I'm all for going green, I'm not in love with losing my pricey hangers. This project came to light because I think despite all of our best intentions to be kind to the planet, somehow wire hangers end up in our closets. So instead of trashing them or wrecking delicate clothes by using them as everyday hangers, I thought this upcycling idea was both cute and functional.

By the way, it's totally up to you if you want to embroider a red heart on the front of each one or not; either way, it's still beautiful.

HOW TO: Place a wire hanger on a piece of ironed cotton-canvas painter's tarp. ✚ Cut out two identical pieces of fabric that are approximately ½ inch larger than the actual hanger, following the shape of the hanger. ✚ Run a bead of fabric glue along both sides of the hanger, following the entire shape of it. ✚ Place the second piece of fabric on top and use your fingers to firmly press the two pieces of fabric together. ✚ Allow to dry for a few hours. ✚ If you want, you can also fray the edges of the fabric-covered hanger for an additional effect.

Here we go with a visit to the Ethicist now: Is it okay to take more than one piece of free candy from the bowl that greets you when you leave the restaurant? Or are we all intended to have just one piece each? Whatever the answer may be, the reality is many of us have cellophane-wrapped candy—fruity or minty—sitting in kitchen drawers or at the bottom of purses just waiting to be upcycled.

HEART-SHAPED RESTAURANT CANDY

SUPPLIES: PURE-SUGAR CANDY (LIKE CLEAR MINTS; NOTHING WITH CREAM, BUTTER, CHOCOLATE; JUST CANDIES MADE WITH SUGAR, FLAVORING AND FOOD COLORING) ✪ HEART-SHAPED SILICONE MOLD ✪ COOKIE SHEET.

HOW TO: Unwrap the candies and place them inside the heart-shaped silicone mold (available at the craft store). Depending on the size of the mold, you'll need about two to four pieces of candy for each one. ✪ Place the mold on top of a cookie sheet and place it inside a 300°F oven; in about 5 minutes, the candy will melt. ✪ Pay attention and make sure to remove the tray when the candy is fully melted, but not bubbling and burning. ✪ Allow to cool completely inside the refrigerator and pop out the finished heart-shaped treats.

When you visit a craft store, there are hundreds of decorative hole punches in a myriad of shapes ranging from basic silhouettes to four-leaf clovers. I'm not a huge believer in investing in all of the choices available, but I do think a heart-shaped puncher comes in handy for a whole variety of projects. Here's just one of many projects where I've found a use for a heart-shaped punch to make a shimmery DIY Valentine's Day love card.

SODA POP LOVE CARDS

SUPPLIES: ALUMINUM SODA CANS ✪ SCISSORS ✪ HEART-SHAPED PUNCH ✪ CRAFT GLUE ✪ BLANK CARDS.

HOW TO: Cut open a soda can using sharp scissors and flatten; rinse and pat dry. ✪ Use a heart-shaped punch to cut out aluminum hearts. ✪ Glue the hearts to the front of cards in whatever pattern you want.

ANOTHER USE FOR HEART-SHAPED PUNCH: Tear out pages from an old book and fold them in half; cut a heart out in the middle, and string them as a novel heart garland.

For me, the words "luxurious" and "bubble bath" go together like peanut butter and jelly or ebony and ivory. Who wouldn't love to soak in a relaxing bubble-filled bathtub on Valentine's Day? And you can give the gift of bubbly beauty with an upcycled homemade concoction that you've whipped up in the kitchen in one easy step. My advice for this project: Smell the little bars of hotel soap before you grate away. Try to mix and match scents that complement each other so the finished result will result in only something oh-so lovely.

GRATED HOTEL-SOAP BUBBLE BATH

SUPPLIES: METAL GRATER ✪ VARIETY OF HOTEL SOAPS ✪ CANNING JARS.

HOW TO: Grate the bars of hotel soap along whatever edge of the grater you want; a finer side will result in finer pieces and a wider one will make bigger soap curls. ✪ Spoon layers of grated soap inside a clean jar; using different colors can create pretty stripes, or go solid if you have enough bars of soap to make one giant jar of bubble-bath soap curls.

JAVA LOVE SCRUB

SUPPLIES: USED COFFEE GRINDS ✪ BROWN SUGAR ✪ ESSENTIAL OIL ✪ CLEAN JELLY-JAM JAR.

One time when I was cleaning the reusable coffee filter in the sink, I scooped some of the grinds into my hands, squeezed a little dish soap in there, and scrubbed away at my rough, dry hands. When I toweled them off, they were smooth and soft. It has become one of my routine beauty treatments whenever I'm hand-washing dishes.

This upcycling project takes it one step further by making an all-over scrub anyone would love. It's been said that the residual caffeine in coffee can help "plump" the skin, meaning the appearance of cellulite can be reduced. If that's actually true, it doesn't matter; the good-for-you scrub will blast dead skin off and leave you feeling baby soft, dimple-free or not.

HOW TO: Start with five parts used coffee and one part sugar (depends on how much coffee you have to start with) and mix them together. ✪ Add a few drops of essential oil—lavender or invigorating peppermint are good choices—and scoop it all into a clean jelly-jam jar. ✪ If you want the striped effect pictured here, skip the mixing part and scoop it all in layers into the jar, adding essential oil drops as you go along.

KID'S T-SHIRT
FABRIC BOWLS

SUPPLIES: OLD KID'S T-SHIRTS ✪ SCISSORS ✪ MOD PODGE GLUE ✪ FOAM BRUSH ✪ METAL MIXING BOWLS ✪ PLASTIC CLING WRAP.

I don't have kids of my own, but I do love my niece and nephew dearly. I'm amazed at how fast they outgrow their adorable clothes. Of course, donating outgrown clothes to Goodwill is a nice way to help others, but that doesn't mean a few strays can't stay behind and be upcycled into these beautiful bowls. So, in case my sister has been wondering where those red, green, and orange T-shirts have gone, no need to worry: they have been refashioned into something almost as cute as her two kids.

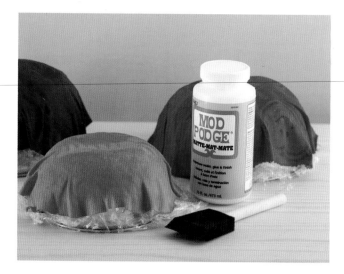

HOW TO: Choose various sizes of metal mixing bowls and turn them upside down. ✪ Wrap them with several layers of plastic cling wrap. ✪ Cut pieces of T-shirts into circles that are large enough to cover the whole bowl, leaving about 1 inch so the shirt doesn't touch the table or work surface. ✪ Liberally apply Mod Podge glue with a foam brush to the front of the T-shirt and drape over the plastic-wrapped bowl. ✪ Apply more glue on top and allow to dry for about an hour. ✪ Add another layer of glue and dry overnight. ✪ When completely dry, remove the T-shirt and peel off the plastic from the hardened fabric bowl. ✪ Use your fingers to crimp the edges if desired.

MESSAGE HOTEL SOAP

SUPPLIES: GLYCERIN HOTEL SOAP ✚ SOAP DYE (FROM MICHAELS CRAFT STORES) ✚ PYREX MEASURING CUP ✚ SILICONE ALPHABET MOLDS

As a road warrior, I've amassed a collection of travel-related things that have become the inspiration for several of my upcycling projects. I personally can't resist taking those little hotel bars of soap—it's like an obsession with me. That means I have a lot of soap at my house—just waiting to be upcycled.

This project is a very easy one to do, but it involves one very important step: You must use pure glycerin soap to make it. Glycerin is the clear type of soap that almost seems to dissolve instantly in your hands in the shower. It's that quick-melting property that makes this project work. If you can't find glycerin soap in your collection of hospitality toiletries, you can also use bars of soap from the drugstore or craft store, too.

HOW TO: Place cut-up pieces of glycerin soap inside a Pyrex measuring cup. ✚ Microwave on high for about 90 seconds and then stir; repeat until the soap is completely melted. ✚ Add a few drops of soap dye—a little goes a long way—and stir. ✚ Pour the soap mixture inside the silicone alphabet mold and allow to cool. If you have a limited amount of soap, only pour it into letter molds that match up to whatever words or phrase you want to spell. ✚ Pop out the letters and arrange to spell whatever message you want, like I HEART YOU or U R DIRTY.

CHOCOLATE CRAYONS

SUPPLIES: RED, BLUE, AND BROWN CRAYON PIECES ✛ SILICONE CANDY MOLDS ✛ VINTAGE OR LEFTOVER CHOCOLATE-CANDY BOX.

When we shot this project for the book, there must've been at least three people on the photo shoot who mistakenly really, truly thought I had made homemade chocolates for them to indulge in. They'd pick up the brown candy-molded crayon, inspect it, and realize this was, in fact, no ordinary candy. In fact, it wasn't candy at all.

Silicone molds are a breakthrough for home bakers the same way the microwave helped cooking-challenged bachelors; nothing sticks to them, they are a cinch to clean, and cookies and candies come out perfect every time.

As an upcycler, it is very much in my DNA to find a new purpose for these molds, and the candy ones are just too hard to resist, to make these upcycled chocolate crayons.

HOW TO: Rummage through old crayons and peel off the paper from red, blue, and brown crayons. ✛ Place pieces inside the silicone mold and melt inside a 300°F oven for about 15 minutes, or until completely melted. ✛ Remove and chill inside the refrigerator for an hour; pop out and arrange inside a chocolate box.

ANOTHER IDEA: Other molds, like these gemstone molds, can be used to make vibrant jeweled crayons, too. Just be sure to use all blue crayons (for "sapphires") or all green (for "emeralds"), etc.

CHAPTER THREE:
BIRTHDAY PARTIES

I originally meant this chapter to be devoted solely to Saint Patrick's Day. But I sat there long and hard thinking about my past Saint Patty's Day activities and it boiled down to two things: hunting for a four-leaf clover in my snow-covered backyard, and downing a green beer at the local O'Houllihan's Bar. Not enough to inspire many upcycling projects perhaps, but the spirit of Saint Patrick's Day is all about having fun and celebrating. So here are my best upcycling ideas for throwing an awesome birthday party, whether you're the birthday guy or girl or hosting a surprise fête for someone else.

Here's what I've discovered over many years of throwing birthday parties: It doesn't matter how old the person is, everyone loves a good party.

We are in festive party mode here: If you like the idea of confetti but hate the mess, this project is definitely for you. Upcycling doesn't get more celebratory than this: Leftover ribbon from previous parties, weddings, and Christmas presents can finally be made into a reusable tablecloth perfect for any occasion. If you don't have a collection of old ribbon you've saved up, flea markets and thrift stores are a great place to find an interesting mix at a fraction of the cost. But if you can, saving up ribbons from special events and making this tablecloth gives you something wonderfully curated; you can tell your guests when and where certain ribbons came from.

RIBBON-CONFETTI TABLECLOTH

SUPPLIES: OLD RIBBON ✪ COTTON PAINTER'S TARP (WASHED AND TUMBLE-DRIED) ✪ IRON ✪ SCISSORS ✪ HEAT-AND-BOND IRON-ON TAPE.

HOW TO: Cut the ribbon pieces into a mix of 1- to 3-inch lengths, mixing it up so there's some variety in the overall design. ✪ Place a piece of the heat-and-bond iron-on tape on the painter's tarp and choose a ribbon piece that fits on top so none of the iron-tape shows. ✪ Place a hot iron on top and let it sit for about 10 seconds so the tape can melt and adhere the ribbon to the fabric. ✪ Continue adding ribbon in a haphazard pattern until the entire tablecloth is covered.

Keeping with the confetti theme, some old wine bottles rummaged out of the recycling bin can be made into festive vases in just a few minutes. If left unadorned, wine bottles filled with flowers would look more downcycled than upcycled. But with the addition of durable and easy-to-work-with duct tape, they take on a whole new look.

FESTIVE WINE-BOTTLE VASES

SUPPLIES: GLASS WINE BOTTLES ✪ DUCT TAPE IN A VARIETY OF COLORS ✪ SCISSORS.

HOW TO: Cut pieces of duct tape into whatever shape you like—squares or rectangular strips—and place them all over the bottle in a random, flurrying pattern.

Inspiration for my projects comes from all sorts of places and sometimes it comes when I least expect it, like eating breakfast with my six-year-old nephew. He was chowing down on Fruit Loops and I was admiring all of the colorful loops of whole grains in the bowl. Why couldn't they be used as beads instead and wired into a large letter as a gift topper? And that's how this project came to be.

MORNING-CEREAL GIFT TOPPERS

SUPPLIES: CEREAL (WE USED FRUIT LOOPS HERE) ✪ SCISSORS ✪ FLORIST WIRE.

HOW TO: Cut a piece of florist wire approximately 24 inches long and bend it into the shape of the letter of your choice. ✪ Twist the wire in places so it stays together in the form of the letter, but keep one main part of it open so you can easily thread cereal onto the wire. ✪ Thread the cereal one at a time and twist the opening closed when you have reached the end.

I don't know why, but the store-bought gift bags—shiny, colorful, screaming HAPPY BIRTHDAY to you—really bother me. First, it was invented for people who don't want to bother with actually wrapping a gift; you just toss the present inside, throw a sheet of tissue paper on top, sign the pre-attached gift tag and *voilà!* Gift. But they cost a lot and are just tossed into the trash right after the party. Here's an easy-to-make, cheap, and prettier version that looks much more thoughtful.

FESTIVE PARTY GIFT BAG

SUPPLIES: PAPER GROCERY-STORE BAG ✪ PINKING SHEARS ✪ RIBBON ✪ HOT-GLUE GUN ✪ ALPHABET STAMP SET AND INKPAD (OPTIONAL).

HOW TO: Cut a grocery-store shopping bag (preferably one not printed with the name of the store on the outside of the bag) in half using pinking shears. ✪ Poke two slits on each side of the bag and run one length of ribbon through each hole to make two loops; glue them to the bag using the hot-glue gun. ✪ Stamp whatever message you want on the front, or leave unadorned.

ROBOT PIÑATA

SUPPLIES: TWO CARDBOARD BOXES ✪ TWO PAPER SHIPPING TUBES ✪ SCISSORS ✪ ROPE ✪ DUCT TAPE ✪ BLACK ELECTRICAL TAPE ✪ OFFICE-SUPPLY STICKERS ✪ MASKING TAPE ✪ CANDY.

I was once at a kid's birthday party and incredibly jealous. Here were small children having the time of their lives swinging a bat at a papier-mâché donkey and all I wanted to do was have my turn, too. I realized that piñatas aren't just for kids, but for adults who aren't just young at heart, but have some aggression they want to work out *and* who'd like to be rewarded with candy.

Traditionally a piñata is a messy process involving glue, wet newspaper, paint, tissue paper, and tons of time. This one eliminated all of that because all you need to do is tape it together.

Also, this upcycling project lends well to the robot shape because of the shape of robots tend to be, well, boxy; if you're particularly crafty, you can tear open a box and mold them into cylinders, balls, or other shapes, too, using scissors and masking tape.

HOW TO: For the box that will be head of the robot, cut a hole at the top of the box and run a piece of rope through the hole and knot it so it rests inside the box and can be hung easily. [See diagram below.] ✪ Fill the boxes with candy and tape them closed with masking tape. ✪ Attach a smaller box on top of a larger box and tape them together using masking tape; it is okay if it's messy-looking because it will all be covered later. ✪ Cut the cardboard tubes into four pieces; two for the arms, two for the legs. ✪ Attach them to the boxes using the masking tape. ✪ Cover everything with layers of duct tape (I used two types here—one matte, one shiny—but you can use whatever you can find). ✪ Decorate the outside with black electrical tape for its facial features, office stickers, whatever you want. ✪ Now swing.

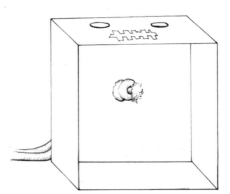

THE UN-BIRTHDAY CAKE

SUPPLIES: VARIETY OF OLD CANDLES ✛ 7-INCH CANDLEWICKS WITH METAL TABS (FROM MICHAELS CRAFT STORES) ✛ LARGE POT AND SMALLER POT (ONE YOU WOULD NO LONGER USE FOR COOKING) AND ANOTHER SMALLER POT FOR WAX STRIPS (OPTIONAL) ✛ METAL CAKE FORM (THIS ONE IS FROM IKEA, BUT ANY METAL CAKE PAN WILL WORK).

I've been to so many birthday parties lately where a giant sheet cake all lit up with candles pretty much goes untouched by all the guests. Is everyone on a juice cleanse? Or Sugar Busters? Whatever the reason, I hate seeing sugary sweets go to waste but also don't want to eliminate the tradition of the birthday boy or girl having a cake with glowing candles to blow out and make a wish. So, call it upcycled or low-carb, this candle birthday "cake" is one low-cal idea to celebrate being one year older.

HOW TO: Simmer water (about 3 inches of water) in a large pot over medium heat and place a smaller pot (one you no longer would use for cooking) inside. ✛ Break old candles into small pieces and place inside that pot and heat until the wax is melted. ✛ Dip each metal-tabbed wick inside the melted wax and place inside the metal cake pan; the wax will help them "stick" to the pan. ✛ Pour a layer of melted wax inside the cake pan about ½ inch at a time. ✛ Allow to cool for about 15 minutes and then and add more wax. ✛ To create a striped effect, have two separate pots of melted wax in different colors ready to go. ✛ Keep pouring until you reach the top. ✛ Cool for 24 hours and then place in the freezer for an hour; this will help the wax pull from the sides of the cake pan so it pops out in one piece.

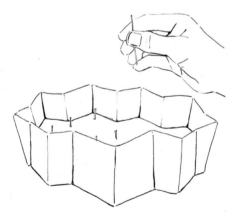

I fear that one day a nutritionist will have an intervention with me and use my books as proof of why I need help: I've used potato-chip bags as gift wrap, to make a faux silver-leafed mirror, and now this: potato-chip-bag balloons.

If you're not a carb-a-holic like I am, you can leave your dignity at the door at any Subway restaurant (preferably after lunch-rush hour), by rolling up your sleeves and pulling out all those chip bags from the trash can. Or you can find a less stare-inducing way to procure them. However you get them, just be sure to give the bags a good washing with warm soapy water so they are totally grease-free.

POTATO-CHIP-BAG BALLOONS

SUPPLIES: SMALL POTATO-CHIP OR SNACK-FOOD BAGS ✪ CRAFT GLUE ✪ COLORED PAPER ✪ HOT-GLUE GUN ✪ STRAWS.

HOW TO: Turn clean chip bags inside-out so the shiny metallic inside is now on the outside. ✪ Stick a straw inside the middle of the bag. Using the hot-glue gun, seal closed the edges on the left and right of the straw. ✪ Blow into the straw to inflate the bag. ✪ Cut out whatever you want from craft paper to attach to the potato-chip-bag balloons (we chose "30" because that was our birthday boy's age) and glue them on using white craft glue.

I don't think I could write an upcycling book on entertaining and not address the fact that many of us still use disposable plates for our parties. I understand their appeal: They are cheap, colorful, and you can toss them into the trash when the party is over. No fuss, no muss. So instead of standing on my soapbox to lecture you about our landfill crisis, I will simply say this: Save the plates from your last disposable bash to make these beautiful flowers for your next party. Just promise me this: Do not go to the store and buy new disposable plates to create this project.

PARTY PLATE FLOWERS

SUPPLIES: LIGHTLY USED LARGE AND SMALL DISPOSABLE-PLASTIC PARTY PLATES ✪ HOLE PUNCH ✪ HOT-GLUE GUN ✪ GUMBALLS ✪ BAMBOO STICKS ✪ DUCT TAPE.

HOW TO: Clean used disposable plates in warm, soapy water and towel dry. Hot glue a smaller plate inside a larger plate. ✪ Use the hole punch to decorate plates. ✪ Hot glue gumballs inside the smaller plate. ✪ Attach a bamboo pole to the back of the plate with duct tape and insert the party plate flowers into the ground.

PLASTIC-BAG FLOWER GIFT TOPPERS

SUPPLIES: PLASTIC SHOPPING BAGS IN DIFFERENT COLORS ✚ DOUBLE-STICK TAPE OR HOT-GLUE GUN WITH GLUE STICKS ✚ SCISSORS.

In the New Year's chapter, there's a tutorial on making plastic shopping bags into poufs that we upcycled into the most charming party lanterns ever. That project idea gets recycled here into a new idea, as gift toppers. So if you want to make these, turn to page 10 for the tutorial.

But for this upcycling gem, the key thing is to use contrasting plastic shopping bags in vibrant colors; mixing blue with yellow or pink and white not only creates a swirl of color, but it also takes on a swirled color-like vibe with the finished result. To attach to the top of the gift, double-stick tape or hot glue will do the trick.

KOOL-AID TIE-DYED GIFT WRAP

SUPPLIES: OLD 100 PERCENT COTTON MEN'S DRESS SHIRT ✪ KOOL-AID PACKETS (SUGAR-FREE, CONCENTRATED) IN A VARIETY OF COLORS ✪ SCISSORS ✪ RUBBER BANDS ✪ RUBBER GLOVES.

I remember watching a TV show as a teenager called *House of Style* on MTV, where the designer Todd Oldham shared a project where he dyed a model's hair with packets of Kool-Aid. That bizarre segment stuck with me because I thought if it's strong enough to dye hair, what else could it do? One day, I had this idea that Kool-Aid could be used in place of toxic fabric dyes to create beautiful colors for fabric. Now, take that idea and imagine me at my local Goodwill store rummaging through a bin of $1 men's white dress shirts, and that's how this came to be.

I discovered shirts that are mixed with polyester don't take on the Kool-Aid as well as 100 percent cotton shirts, so take a look at the labels inside. And I also discovered that not wearing rubber gloves leaves your hands dyed with tropical punch, cherry, and grape stains. Stains, I might add, that are very hard to remove without the aid of bleach. So make the small investment in rubber gloves before you tackle this one.

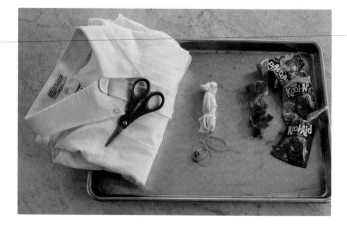

HOW TO: Cut the men's dress shirt into pieces—two sleeves as wine-bottle gift wrap and squares of fabric for traditional wrap—and soak in cold water. ✪ Fold, twist, and roll the fabric however you want and add rubber bands as you go along to help create the tie-dye effect. ✪ Make sure the rubber bands are twisted tightly onto the fabric. ✪ While wearing rubber gloves, open packets of Kool-Aid and sprinkle them onto the fabric. Be generous with it and use your fingers to press the fabric so the dye penetrates it completely; you can squeeze it as hard as you can to really make sure the color is fully saturated. ✪ Mix and match different colors to create gradient colors. ✪ Use scissors to cut the rubber bands, and lay the fabric flat so it can air dry. ✪ You can rinse the fabric, but the fabric will look more faded; keeping it un-rinsed has the yummy side effect of the fabric smelling like tropical fruit punch.

CHAPTER FOUR:
SPRING CELEBRATIONS

I often think my thrill for flea markets may be traced back to my early years as a child on Easter Sunday: waking up early, grabbing a basket, and hunting throughout the house for hidden plastic Easter eggs filled with treats and small treasures. It was the thrill of the hunt that made it memorable and fun, just the same way it's thrilling to hunt for treasures at the flea market. And even though one year plastic eggs evolved into real dyed eggs, I still loved the tradition of searching for the eggs despite not loving the taste of hard-boiled eggs at all.

In addition to the religious reasons for celebrating Easter or Passover, it's also the time we can celebrate the withering of winter and the arrival of spring. Crocuses peeking out of the snow-covered ground; buds appearing on barren dogwood branches; days becoming longer and nights being, well, not as cold. Yet I find it incredibly frustrating to see disposable bags of plastic eggs, fake grass, cheap baskets, and bad-tasting candy in stores. I figured there were others who found the fake grass, well, crass, and I knew there were some clever upcycling solutions to this environmental abomination. Here are some ideas to make your springtime a little more green.

GARDEN-HOSE EASTER BASKET

SUPPLIES: OLD (BUT CLEAN) GARDEN HOSE APPROXIMATELY 10 FEET IN LENGTH ✚ 10 TO 15 WHITE PLASTIC ZIP TIES (8 INCH TIES) ✚ SCISSORS.

Not all of my fellow crafters I would say are also eco-minded. If given the option of sorting through a recycling bin for materials or shopping the aisles of a clean, well-lit store, they would choose retail stores for sure. Which is why when I handed them a dirty old garden hose and some zip ties, they wondered what I had up my crafting sleeves. But for even the most jaded non recycler stylist, there are gem projects in this book that I've seen inspire them to rethink this whole upcycling thing altogether. This is one of them.

Who would've thought those two items could be used to make the plumpest, coolest looking basket ever? And a durable basket with a myriad of uses, whether it's used to fill up with eggs at an Easter-egg hunt or filled with potting soil as a truly functional outdoor planter.

HOW TO: Coil the end of a garden hose to create the base, using zip ties every 6 to 8 inches to bind two pieces of hose together. ✚ Once you achieve the base size you want, start bringing up the hose to build the actual basket, adding more zip ties as you go along to secure it together. ✚ When you get to the top of the basket, use the remaining hose length to make the handle, and zip-tie it securely onto the basket. This may take some practice, but there will be no need to use scissors to cut the hose whatsoever; you'll just need them to trim the zip ties so the finished look is clean and simple.

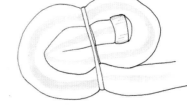

PLASTIC EGG-CARTON MINI GREENHOUSE

SUPPLIES: CLEAR PLASTIC EGG CARTON ✪ POTTING SOIL ✪ SEEDS.

Easter to me isn't just a festive holiday, but it's a mark of warmer weather to come. As backyard gardening continues to rise in popularity, one way to grow homegrown (and hopefully organic!) fresh produce is to start seedlings right at home. Plastic egg cartons are the perfect way to do this.

This upcycling idea is not so much a craft project rather a smart repurposing idea. But what I love about it is that kids can get involved and watch seeds germinate over time. In a world where we covet instant gratification, I think it's important to embrace activities that evolve and require a little patience. This is one easy way to slow down and get your green thumb growing.

HOW TO: In a clean plastic egg carton, fill the inside compartment with potting soil. ✪ Mist with water and insert seeds in each compartment. ✪ Mist liberally again and close the lid. ✪ Place in a warm, sunny spot and watch the seeds come to life.

I once dyed eggs using natural ingredients like beets, turmeric, and other supermarket items I would never eat. The process of figuring out how to create vibrantly colored eggs without the use of artificial dyes was—to say the least— time-consuming, frustrating, and often with uneven results. If spending hours boiling beets isn't for you, don't give up quite yet.

Here's a project for those of us who want Easter-egg dyeing to be all about less work and more impact. If you're a coffee drinker, make an extra-big pot that morning, and use whatever is left over to get this going *after* you've been properly caffeinated.

MORNING-JAVA-DYED EGGS

SUPPLIES: LEFTOVER COFFEE ✪ WHITE EGGS ✪ OFFICE-SUPPLY STICKERS.

HOW TO: Bring a dozen eggs out of the refrigerator in room temperature for about an hour before you make this project; cold eggs do not hold stickers well. ✪ Place office-supply stickers—we used small dots—all over the outside of the egg in whatever pattern you want. ✪ Press firmly so the stickers are well adhered. ✪ Slip each egg into a hot pot of coffee and place back into the coffeemaker; leave the coffeemaker on so the coffee stays hot (this will also hard-boil the eggs for you, but they will not be safe enough to eat). ✪ About 90 minutes later, remove the eggs and rinse under cool tap water to cool. ✪ Peel off stickers.

Even though I try to be a stickler about bringing my own reusable bags to the grocery store, there will be those last-minute trips where you need to choose: paper or plastic. I usually opt for paper because I can reuse the bag at home for a myriad of purposes. This one is one of the easiest and prettiest: an oversized egg placemat.

I envisioned this as an upcycling project I could do with my niece and nephew: as their uncle, I'd cut the bag for them and they could go to town decorating it. You can also re-envision this project for other holidays: imagine an oversized Christmas ball or pumpkin for Halloween, too.

OVERSIZED EGG PLACEMAT

SUPPLIES: GROCERY-STORE BROWN PAPER BAG ✪ TISSUE PAPER ✪ SCISSORS ✪ CRAFT GLUE.

HOW TO: Use scissors to cut open the grocery bag so it's one large, flat piece of brown craft paper. ✪ Cut out two egg silhouettes. ✪ Decorate with tissue paper and use white craft glue to attach to the paper.

CRYSTALLIZED EASTER "FLOWERS"

SUPPLIES: SPRING-COLORED SILK FLOWERS ⊕ BORAX LAUNDRY BOOSTER ⊕ PLASTIC CONTAINER (THIS ONE IS FROM CHINESE-FOOD TAKEOUT) ⊕ WOODEN CHOPSTICKS ⊕ FLORIST WIRE ⊕ HOT WATER.

Silk flowers are one of those craft-store items I once said I would never, ever buy. But like the saying "never say never," I have to change my rule by saying I will never, ever buy *new* silk flowers. The reason? Goodwill and other thrift stores are usually overrun with bags of dusty old artificial flora and they sell them for next to nothing. So, being the altruistic crafter I am, I wanted to come up with a project that helped these great give-back stores unload merchandise, all while giving us upcyclers a reason to stock up on some plastic stems. The end results are crystallized flowers that look like diamond-encrusted bouquets.

HOW TO: Attach a single stem of silk flower to a chopstick (or a twig if you don't have any chopsticks) using florist wire. ⊕ Insert it into a clean plastic container (save soup containers from takeout) and make sure when the chopstick rests on top of the container, the flower is not touching the sides or bottom. ⊕ Remove the flower and fill the container with very hot water from the sink. ⊕ Stir in five tablespoons of Borax and mix until it is completely dissolved. ⊕ Repeat the process to crystallize all of the flowers. ⊕ Insert the flower and leave somewhere where it will be undisturbed for at least 24 hours. ⊕ After 24 hours, lift the flower to find your crystallized flowers. ⊕ Allow the flowers to air-dry on a towel, and arrange.

SILHOUETTE EASTER-BASKET FLOWER ARRANGEMENT

SUPPLIES: COLORFUL CRAFT-PAPER CARDSTOCK ✪ X-ACTO KNIFE ✪ SCISSORS ✪ PLASTIC CUP ✪ STRING.

I get the inspiration for my upcycling projects from my day-to-day interactions in life. So, if I were a serious bowler, you'd probably see lots of upcycled items using bowling balls and beer bottles. But alas, I am not. Instead, my daily routine involves a run to my local Starbucks, but what pains me when I'm there are the overflowing trash cans full of barely used plastic cups that once held a mocha-frap-iced-skim whatever.

So one day I grabbed a few, washed them really well, and tried to figure out a simple but functional way to upcycle them. Instead of slicing, dicing, shredding, and manipulating the plastic cups, I just used them for what they did best: hold liquids. This silhouette-basket flower arrangement is what I came up with.

HOW TO: First, finish up your iced coffee and save the cup. Clean it well and dry it with a towel. ✪ Now that you're caffeinated and alert, grab a sheet of craft-paper cardstock and sketch out the shape of a basket on the white side of the paper. If you're not good with freehand, you can find a silhouette image online, print it out, and use it as a template. ✪ When you're happy with the design, cut it out using scissors and an X-Acto knife. ✪ Attach the plastic cup to the back of the basket and tie secure with white string so it wraps around the cup and onto the front of the basket. ✪ Fill the cup with water and arrange a spring bouquet of Mother Nature's finest flowers.

SUSTAINABLE EASTER GRASS

SUPPLIES: PAPER FROM THE RECYCLING BIN ✚ GREEN CRAFT PAINT ✚ BRUSH ✚ PAPER SHREDDER.

Despite my fear about sounding like an old man who yells at squirrels for poaching birdseed and then somehow segues it into the high cost of gas, I'm gonna stand on my soapbox and say this: What is the deal with artificial Easter grass sold in stores?

While there are some new biodegradable faux Easter grasses that you can special order online, the majority of the bags of fake turf sold in stores are made from plastic. Correction: It is non biodegradable, petroleum-based, landfill-clogging material, all to simply fill a basket so the chocolate Easter bunny has somewhere fluffy to rest. It's an outrage!

While real grass from the yard isn't an option for most (can't imagine any of you want to spend your early morning clipping grass with scissors), this upcycling idea is ideal for those of us looking for a greener alternative.

HOW TO: Simply take sheets of paper destined for the recycling bin and paint a thin layer of green craft paint on top (no need to be perfect here; just make sure you paint the majority of the paper). Let it dry completely. ✚ Then run it through a paper shredder and voilà! Grass.

PLASTIC-SPOON TULIP ARRANGEMENT

SUPPLIES: COLORFUL PLASTIC SPOONS ⊕ TWINE ⊕ TERRA COTTA POT ⊕ STYROFOAM (FROM PACKAGING) ⊕ MOSS.

I call this a tulip arrangement even though there are no tulips in it and the only arranging you have to do is jab some spoons into a block of foam. But let me start off with this urgent request: Please do not go to the store and buy a box of brand new plastic spoons to make this project. Instead, save them from when you do actually use them at a party, clean them, and upcycle them so that you can be both stylish and sustainable at the same time.

I just love this project because these spoons grouped together really do look like flowers emerging from the ground, but with a whimsical twist. You know they are plastic spoons and not for a second would anyone think they're real, but that's the point: They're faux flowers that are really fun as fakes.

HOW TO: Cut a piece of Styrofoam to fit snug inside the terra cotta pot you're using for the project. ⊕ Group three or four spoons together and tie twine around the neck of the spoons. ⊕ Adjust so they take on the look of a closed tulip blossom. ⊕ Jab each plastic flower into the Styrofoam. ⊕ Decorate the top with some craft-store moss.

Not sure if upcycled peppers are really relevant to Easter, but they are so cute you'll want to adopt a new tradition and have these alongside your chocolate bunnies and sugary chicks in your Easter basket.

PLASTIC PEPPER TREAT POTS

SUPPLIES: GREEN PLASTIC SODA OR WATER BOTTLES ✪ JELLY BEANS ✪ CLEAR SCOTCH TAPE ✪ SCISSORS ✪ PIPE CLEANERS ✪ PENCIL ✪ HOT-GLUE GUN.

HOW TO: Cut several plastic water bottles in half using sharp scissors. You'll need two bottles to make one plastic pepper. ✪ Rinse the bottles in warm, soapy water in the sink and dry them completely with a towel. ✪ Trim each bottle half even further, so it's just a few inches up from the base of the bottle. ✪ Fill a dry half with jelly beans (or any candy you want) and invert the other bottle half on top so it's snug; one bottle piece will fit slightly inside the other. ✪ Secure a few pieces of clear Scotch Tape around the perimeter to ensure a tight closure. ✪ Wrap a pipe cleaner around a pencil to make it curly like a stem; remove the pencil, and attach using hot glue.

Earlier in this chapter, I shared a project that takes an old grocery-store paper bag and makes it into a kid-friendly Easter egg placemat. Now it's time for a more grown-up place setting for your traditional Easter lunch or dinner.

In reality, you could make these placemats and use them all-year round. There's nothing screaming Easter about them, but I thought this upcycling project seemed completely appropriate for this chapter. Usually for Sunday brunch, men wear their nicest, preppiest dress shirts, so I guess an old Sunday-best shirt should be upcycled into a placemat. If you don't have shirts, our go-to store—Goodwill—will surely have a nice selection for you to choose from.

MEN'S-SHIRT PLACEMATS

SUPPLIES: MEN'S DRESS SHIRTS ✪ PINKING SHEARS ✪ IRON ✪ A VISIT TO THE LOCAL COPY SHOP.

HOW TO: With sharp pinking shears, cut out a rectangular piece of fabric from the back of the dress shirt in the size of the desired placemat. If you're using a plaid shirt (as pictured here), use the pattern of the shirt as guidelines to cut neat, straight lines. ✪ When you're done cutting all the placemats, use an iron to press them neat and flat. ✪ Bring them to a copy shop that can laminate oversized items, and request a clear laminate. ✪ Use the pinking shears to trim the laminated placemats.

GLOSSY PAINT-CHIP ID TAGS

SUPPLIES: PAINT CHIPS ⊙ SCISSORS ⊙ FOAM BRUSH ⊙ MOD PODGE GLOSS GLUE ⊙ HOLE PUNCH ⊙ RING BINDER CLIP.

In 2002, I decided to leave New York City and give living in rural Pennsylvania a try. But before I dove in and bought a home, I had decided to rent a place and see if the slower pace of the Keystone State really appealed to me.

I rented a 500-acre Christmas-tree farm outside of Reading, Pennsylvania, and fell in love. Here, I could create projects, write books, and produce stories for magazines, all from a quiet, idyllic home that overlooked neat rows of Christmas trees.

On Easter one year, I was invited by the owner of the farm to come celebrate with them. Several bottles of champagne later, I realized everyone's glasses (all identical) were mixed up, except for a few lipstick-stained ones. It was then and there that I thought there has to be a simple way to keep track of your glasses so stray bubbly is, well, no longer astray. Since it is such a shame to waste good champers, I came up with this pastel-colored project using a variety of materials and crafting tools we all have.

HOW TO: Choose Easter-colored paint chips and cut them down to smaller sizes using sharp scissors. ⊙ Dip your foam brush into the Mod Podge gloss glue and cover the outside of the chip. ⊙ Apply several layers and allow to dry; it will dry to an almost glass-like finish that will also add durability to the paint chip. ⊙ Punch a hole with a hole punch and attach to the glasses using a ring binder clip (from the office-supply store). ⊙ If you want to personalize them, use a permanent marker to write the guest's name on each wineglass ID tag.

Wild Grape
C1 212

UPCYCLED SEDER PLATE

SUPPLIES: 6 SMALL PLATES (OR SAUCERS) ✚ 5 METAL SPOONS ✚ E-6000 GLUE.

For those who celebrate Passover, a Seder plate can be a difficult item to find in stores. But with a little creativity and time, you can upcycle one that will be perfect to showcase the symbolic foods at your Passover Seder.

HOW TO: Flip each plate upside down and clean the surface with an all-purpose cleaner and towel. ✚ Squeeze a dab of E-6000 glue on the back of a spoon and attach to the back of one of the outer plates; add another drop of E-6000 glue to the handle of the same spoon and attach it to the center plate's back. ✚ Repeat all around to create a celestial pattern with the plates. ✚ Dry overnight.

Flip the entire Seder plate and arrange individual ingredients onto each plate: The "Charoset" (mixture of chopped apples, nuts, red wine, cinnamon); "Marror" (a bitter herb usually represented with horseradish root); "Chazeret" (another bitter herb usually represented by romaine lettuce); "Z'roa" (shank bone; ask your local butcher to save one for you); "Karpas" (green vegetable or herb, usually parsley, dipped in salt water); "Beitzah" (a hard-boiled egg).

CHAPTER FIVE:
MOTHER'S AND FATHER'S DAY

Yes, I'm grouping these holidays together because, frankly, I think they should just be *one* holiday to begin with. Isn't it enough I have to remember my parents' birthdays, anniversary, all the major holidays, the day they immigrated to the United States (seriously), *and* then we need a whole other holiday to celebrate the fact that they created me? They brought me into this world together, so why can't I gift them a token of thanks together? Well, at least I can group ideas to celebrate our parents into one chapter.

Ranting aside, the upcycling projects in this chapter are pretty interchangeable between either parent. With families now having two moms or two dads, and with all the variations of single parenting, coparenting, and step-parenting, I prefer to leave the choice of gift to you, the upcycler.

There's no need to interpret a project exactly as given, too. The solid perfume project may seem like a great Mom gift since it involves fragrance, but what if the dad in question travels a lot on business? He surely could use a TSA-friendly solid cologne to go? It's the process and idea that I really want to share, and your knowledge of the recipient and their likes and dislikes makes it a gift you make all your own.

COLOR-STRIPED
REUSABLE TOTE BAG

SUPPLIES: DUCT TAPE IN VARIOUS COLORS ✛ SCISSORS ✛ REUSABLE TOTE BAG.

There are two things that drive me nuts at stores. Right there at check-out, as if to respond to the Green Movement, are those 99 cent reusable tote bags emblazoned with their store logo. Sure, the bags are cheap to buy, but they are awfully flimsy and a walking advertisement for the purchaser to carry. While I encourage the use of reusable bags, the problem with these bags is two-fold: They barely last and are not so attractive to look at.

This project solves both problems in one easy step, because the duct tape reinforces the bag and it conceals all of the obnoxious branding on the front of the bag. Choose duct tape in multiple colors; lots of stripes in complementary colors look cool and it's very fashion-forward in appearance.

HOW TO: Flatten the reusable bag so the sides bend in and you're working with a flat piece of fabric. ✛ Run a strip of duct tape (starting at the top) across the front with about 3 to 4 inches of tape overlapping the sides of the bag. ✛ Then carefully fold the duct tape pieces around the bag so they evenly adhere to the sides of the bag. ✛ Repeat with a different color of tape until you reach the bottom. ✛ Flip the bag and repeat the whole process again on the other side, and make sure the ends of the tape meet or overlap the strips you made on the front. ✛ Be sure to press the tape down firmly to get a nice, flat finish.

HOMEMADE OIL
AND VINEGAR BOTTLES

SUPPLIES: CLEAN WINE BOTTLES ⊙ DRY-ERASE BOARD PAINT ⊙ BRUSH ⊙ PAINTER'S TAPE ⊙ BOTTLE POUR SPOUTS ⊙ HOMEMADE CONCOCTION OF OIL OR VINEGAR ⊙ RIBBON (OPTIONAL).

I'm not even going to offer the slightest clue how to make your own infused oils and vinegar because there are far better cookbooks, websites, and tips from your friends on how to do this. But what I will do is show you a very clever way to upcycle a charming wine bottle with a bit of dry-erase paint to make something pretty professional looking that can make so-so vinegars and oils look gourmet-store worthy.

If you're wondering what dry-erase board paint is, think about any corporate board room or college classroom. It's that white, shiny board you can write all over with a special marker and wipe off with an eraser. Dry-erase paint is just like chalkboard paint except for dry-erase markers: You paint on a few coats and voilà! You can have a dry-erase board anywhere you want. Feel free to customize the bottles with whatever you want, and add a festive ribbon to make it a gift anyone would love.

HOW TO: Wash the wine bottle and hand dry as well as you can. ⊙ Place the bottles (laying flat) in a 350°F oven and let them "bake" for one hour; this will sterilize the bottles. ⊙ Turn off the oven and allow the bottles to cool inside (overnight if you can). ⊙ Tape off a section of the bottle you want to have the dry-erase paint strip on. ⊙ Paint several light coats of paint and allow to dry. ⊙ Fill the bottles with your homemade concoction of oil or vinegar, insert a bottle pour spout on top, and write a message on the dry-erase painted part of the bottle. ⊙ Tie a ribbon around the neck of the bottle if desired.

NYLON REUSABLE TOTE-BAG GIFT WRAP

SUPPLIES: NYLON REUSABLE BAGS (THESE ARE BAGGU BRAND)

✛ SAFETY PIN.

I don't think I could write a chapter about Mother's and Father's Day gifts without including an idea for gift wrap. Sure, you could make something nice and just hand it to your parents with a smile, but gift wrap is all part of the allure and surprise of giving. But with the waste that comes from the paper and ribbon; surely there has to be a greener way?

This is one of my favorite ideas because the recipient really gets two gifts instead of one. All you have to do is place the gift inside the bag, fold the excess fabric at the bottom of the gift and pin it with a safety pin. Then use the handles to make your bow on top. When the gift is open, they are also left with a fabulous reusable bag.

My friends will confirm this: I cannot show up to a dinner party with a bare bottle of wine in my hands. It has to be wrapped. I think the reason boils down to a little enforced rule about walking around in public with a bottle of alcohol that's not concealed in a bag. And since I don't like disposable plastic and paper bags, I always show up with an upcycled wrapped bottle of wine.

As far as my own dad goes, I know there are two gifts that will actually be appreciated: a good bottle of vino or Scotch, and a nice designer silk necktie. So instead of choosing, I get to surprise him twice with this winner.

MEN'S NECKTIE-WRAPPED WINE BOTTLE

SUPPLIES: GOOD BOTTLE OF WINE OR SPIRITS ✪ SILK TIE ✪ TIE CLIP OR LARGE SAFETY PIN.

HOW TO: This project could not be simpler: just wrap the tie around the bottle, starting at the bottom and working your way up. ✪ Make sure the tie is taut against the bottle and then clip it in place at the top with a tie clip or safety pin.

BEACH BODY SCRUBBY SOAP

SUPPLIES: GLYCERIN SOAP (FROM MICHAELS CRAFT STORES) ⊕ MICROWAVEABLE CONTAINER (PYREX MEASURING CUPS) ⊕ SPOON ⊕ BEACH SAND ⊕ SOAP DYE ⊕ A WAXY CONTAINER (FROM MILK OR ORANGE JUICE) ⊕ SCISSORS ⊕ KNIFE.

I was once in a very fancy department store where the address of the store was also its name (I am guessing that by the, um, *fifth* guess—hint hint—you'll figure it out) where I saw a bar of soap for sale. On one end was a sandy-like surface and the other end was clear, pure glycerin soap. A tiny little bar of this scrubby soap was $15. I knew this was an upcycling challenge I could re-create for less.

My hope for those of you who make this project is that you'll use sand that ends up in the bottom of your tote bag or shoes when you're at the shore, since taking sand from the beach would only contribute to erosion. Our beaches need sand to prevent erosion and as silly as it sounds, even pilfering a small amount is doing a little bit of harm. So, if a weekend at the Jersey Shore isn't on your agenda, you can buy sand from a home-improvement store or even raid your kid's sand pit at home. To sterilize it, just place it inside a shallow baking dish (aluminum works fine) at 300°F for about an hour.

HOW TO: Cut a juice or milk container in half and wash with warm, soapy water; dry with a towel. ⊕ Melt the glycerin soap in a microwavable container (Pyrex measuring cups work well) according to package instructions; stir it every few minutes until it's completely melted. ⊕ Pour about ¼ to ½ of a cup of sand into the container, then pour the melted soap on top. Stir. ⊕ Add a few drops of soap dye of your choice. ⊕ Cool in the refrigerator for an hour. ⊕ Peel the wax container open and slice the soap with a knife.

CUSTOMIZED SOLID PERFUME

SUPPLIES: BEESWAX ✪ PERFUME ✪ JOJOBA OIL ✪ SMALL MINT OR CANDY TIN.

Spray perfumes are like the SUVs of beauty: they aren't really an efficient use of what they have; you spray the perfume and the majority of it ends up in the air or on your clothes and not on your skin. The beauty of solid perfumes is that they can last an incredibly long time, there's very little waste, and they are TSA-friendly to travel with. Instead of spraying your favorite scent haplessly into the air, with a solid perfume you can apply the scent directly to the skin and at the exact pulse points you want.

Turning any spray scent into a solid perfume is incredibly simple. The trick to make the end result for this project feel more special is to source a gorgeous candy tin. I shopped for Italian tins at New York City's famed Eataly, but any specialty or import food store should offer you a nice selection to choose from.

HOW TO: There are two ways to melt beeswax: One, you can chop up small pieces and melt it over a double boiler in a clean Pyrex measuring cup. Two, you can simply light a beeswax pillar candle an hour before you start this project. I prefer the latter because you'll get the nice scent of beeswax in the air and there's no clean-up at the end. ✪ Start by cleaning the mint tin with soapy water; even a trace smell of peppermint can interfere with perfume, so it's best to be slightly obsessive-compulsive about making sure it's clean and dry. ✪ Then tip the beeswax candle so the melted wax pours inside the tin about three-fourths of the way up; squirt about 25 or 30 sprays of perfume and stir. ✪ Add three drops of jojoba oil (helps to preserve it) and allow to cool. ✪ Apply to skin with your fingers.

MOTHER NATURE'S BEST POTPOURRI

SUPPLIES: ITEMS FROM NATURE LIKE TREE BARK, SEA SHELLS, SEA GLASS, RIVER ROCKS, AND TWIGS ✪ ESSENTIAL OILS ✪ BOWL.

As a child, I had a visceral reaction when it came to potpourri and I don't know why. Maybe it had something to do with the fact that dried, dead flowers were deeply dyed and saturated with a woodsy-piney-floral fragrance that you could easily smell through the thick cellophane bag. Or maybe because I couldn't understand why someone would want to fill a bowl with this stuff and leave it in your house to begin with.

But as I got older, I started to enjoy having fragrance in my own home from homemade sprays, and I also liked decorating with found objects I would scour from the great outdoors. This project is a marriage of those two loves, and I think is an updated and acceptable version of potpourri.

HOW TO: All you have to do is find beautiful objects at the beach, or strips of wood from a birch tree, or along a river bank. ✪ Be considerate and take only what you need. ✪ Toss the clean natural materials with lots of essential oil in your favorite scent. ✪ And display in a bowl to admire and smell.

UPCYCLED METALLIC HOTEL PENS

SUPPLIES: DISPOSABLE PLASTIC PENS ✪ FLORIST WIRE ✪ SCISSORS ✪ ALUMINUM ELECTRICAL TAPE.

I actually will admit this: I have stayed at Le Parker Meridien Hotel in New York City not because of their excellent service, roomy rooms, or central location. I have intentionally stayed there so I can replenish my stock of their guest-room pens.

Whether or not you share my obsession with a hotel pen, many of us have a stockpile of plastic disposable pens advertising a chain hotel, restaurant, real estate agent, or whatever. Perfectly functional but often pretty ugly, you can upcycle a small collection into a whimsical arrangement of writing utensils using pressed aluminum tape from the hardware store.

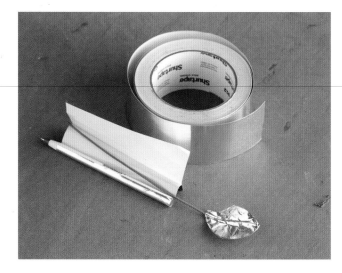

HOW TO: Start by measuring a 4- to 5-inch length of florist wire and cutting it with sharp scissors. ✪ Place 2 inches of the wire along the edge of the pen and wrap aluminum tape around it and the pen to secure it into place, until you get to the end of the pen. ✪ Wrap the whole pen in aluminum tape, pressing with your fingers as you go along to smooth it into place. ✪ Sandwich several squares of aluminum tape on top of the exposed wire at the end of the pen and use scissors to cut the tape into whatever shape you want (we did a leaf).

WEARABLE POCKET-WATCH FRAME

SUPPLIES: POCKET WATCH ✚ PORTRAIT PHOTO ✚ BLUNT KNIFE (LIKE A BUTTER KNIFE) ✚ RIBBON (OPTIONAL).

There are two things I know about pocket watches: I don't know anyone who wears them and I also see them for sale all the time at flea markets. You may have some vintage pocket watches at home, but if not, you can find them for a few dollars at swap meets and thrift shops. Don't think *Antiques Roadshow*–worthy watches for this project; think metal cases, interesting designs, and more sentimental than monetary value.

HOW TO: The hardest part will be prying open the back of the pocket watch. For some watches, it's as easy as twisting the back with your fingers. For others, you'll need to finesse it a bit to pry off the back with the help of a blunt butter knife. There is usually a small indentation somewhere on the back where you can pry it open. Be patient; I promise, you will eventually find a way to open it.

Once open, remove all the inner works of the watch until you just have the crystal front still in place. ✚ Cut the photo you want to put inside to size, and place inside and put the cover back on top. ✚ You can wear as is or replace the chain with a grosgrain ribbon.

I may have confessed that I am a lazy crafter, but don't confuse my hyperefficiency with "phoning" it in. When it comes to greeting cards, I don't like e-cards (too impersonal) or store-bought cards (the price tag is printed on the back *and* the greeting is already printed inside!). I like to make my own cards and give them to the recipients.

If the idea of making your own cards all-year round is giving you the chills, what about celebrating your mother *and* Mother Earth by making just *one* card *once* a year? This project is easy and eco, and one that will end up on prime real estate on your mother's refrigerator come Mother's Day.

LEAF FRAMED CARDS

SUPPLIES: PRESSED LEAVES FROM THE YARD ✪ GENERIC CARD STOCK ✪ PHOTOS ✪ GLUE.

HOW TO: Collect leaves from the yard and press them between pages of heavy books. ✪ If you collect already dried-out leaves from the ground that are not brittle to the touch, the pressing process will take days instead of weeks. ✪ Decorate card stock with leaves and photos as you wish.

For Mom

When I moved to New York City in my early twenties, two things were certain: rent was due at the first of the month and I would always come home to a pile of Chinese food menus under my door.

Whether you use them to order food or not, paper menus are a ubiquitous junk drawer staple. And while I have this upcycling project slotted as a Mother's Day gift (thinking it would be a fun and functional project for a child to make), it can actually be a rather useful accessory during the hot summer months, too. Make a bunch, display in a jar or vase, and let your guests fan themselves.

CHINESE TAKEOUT MENU FANS

SUPPLIES: 3–5 TAKEOUT MENUS ⊕ HOT-GLUE GUN WITH GLUE STICKS ⊕ 2 WOODEN PAINT STIRRERS ⊕ RIBBON (OPTIONAL) ⊕ CRAFT PAINT (OPTIONAL).

HOW TO: Paint the wooden stirrers a coordinating color if desired and allow to dry. ⊕ Open the takeout menu so it's one flat piece and begin to fold it accordion style lengthwise from one end to another; each fold is about 1 inch wide. ⊕ Repeat this with 3 to 4 more menus. ⊕ Fold the folded menu in half so it looks like a "V" shape and glue the inner flaps so it looks like ¼ of the folded fan. ⊕ Repeat and attach all the "V"s together until it creates a circular fan. ⊕ Hot glue two matching ends of the paint stirrers together and hot glue the ends to the middle of the fan. Add ribbon if desired.

DOTTED GLASSWARE VASES

SUPPLIES: CHIPPED GLASSWARE ✚ EMPTY GLASS CONTAINERS ✚ PAINTER'S TAPE ✚ PEBEO PORCELAINE GLAZE IN THE FINE TIP TUBE (AT MICHAELS CRAFT STORES) ✚ FLORAL OR FILIGREE PAPER ✚ SCISSORS.

As you may know, I like upcycling projects that have a beautiful finished result that looks like it took a lot of skill and time but in actuality, took just minutes to make. The beauty of what I call "fast and flashy" upcycling is that you can make a whole bunch of the same project in very little time and group them together for dramatic effect. Or, you can make a whole bunch and gift them individually to lots of people.

And if you're looking at these beautiful vases with intricate flowers, filigrees, and designs and think you don't have the artistic prowess to pull it off, think again: if you can trace a line, you can make these beauties, too.

HOW TO: Raid your pantry, recycling bin, or kitchen cabinets for glassware you aren't using. Think jelly jars, water glasses, and champagne flutes with a small chip. Use glassware that is free of any embellishment and has a nice clean, clear surface all over.

Cut a piece of floral or filigree patterned paper (we used old gift wrap) and cut it to fit snug inside the glass piece; tape it along the edges of the glass to make sure it's secure and won't move around inside the glass. ✚ Then follow the pattern on the outside of the glass by adding drops of the Porcelaine glaze all over, one at a time. ✚ When done, remove the paper on the inside to reveal the pattern. ✚ To set the glaze dots, put them into a cold oven on a baking sheet. ✚ Turn it on at 350°F and bake for 10–15 minutes. ✚ Turn off the oven and allow them to cool fully inside.

WORLD'S BEST MOM OR DAD TROPHY

SUPPLIES: RANDOM HOUSEHOLD OBJECTS (BOOKS, MUG, BINDER CLIPS, JAR LIDS, ETC.) ⊕ GOLD SPRAY PAINT ⊕ E-6000 GLUE ⊕ HOT-GLUE GUN ⊕ CHALKBOARD PAINT (OPTIONAL) ⊕ CHALK (OPTIONAL).

It may not be an Academy Award or a Grammy, but this upcycled trophy will still earn prime real estate in your home because it's definitely one-of-a-kind. Kids will have a great time creating this trophy because it's one part scavenger hunt, one part building and gluing, and one part transformation in a quick and easy project. Depending on their age, they will probably need help with gluing and painting, but let them go wild finding stray things to build their own award-winning masterpiece.

HOW TO: It doesn't matter what color the objects are that you're using to make this upcycled trophy; a few coats of metallic spray paint will unify everything to make it look like one casted piece. ⊕ Start with the base: think heavy, sturdy objects like old books or a wooden cigar box. ⊕ Then build it up with a coffee mug as the center vessel, maybe propped up with a collection of Army men figurines or paper clips. ⊕ Keep playing around until you're happy with your design and glue it all together, using E-6000 for the heavier, bigger sections that are being glued together and hot glue to add small details and touches. ⊕ Allow to dry and spray paint (in a well ventilated area) with a few coats of metallic paint. ⊕ If you want a chalkboard plaque to personalize with a message, paint a jar lid with two coats of black chalkboard paint and glue to the front.

COFFEE BAG BASKET

SUPPLIES: ABOUT 6–8 PLASTIC/FOIL COFFEE BAGS ✪ SCISSORS ✪ CARDBOARD ✪ DUCT TAPE OR ELECTRICAL ALUMINUM TAPE.

If it's shade-grown, USDA-certified organic, Rainforest Alliance–approved, locally roasted coffee, but it comes in one of those unrecyclable plastic/foil bags, is it eco-friendly? While a purist response would be to simply kick the caffeine habit, the addict in me says it's green because I can upcycle the bags into a durable coffee bag basket.

Once this upcycled basket is made, there are a ton of uses for it: fill it with bags of coffee, doughnuts, mugs, and other Java Lover essentials and give it as a gift. Or throw it on the floor by your favorite place to curl up and read and fill with books and magazines. Even rolling up some towels and stacking them inside the bathroom could look super chic.

HOW TO: Start with the circumference of the basket. Depending how large you want the basket, you'll need about 6 to 8 coffee bags for this project. ✪ Using sharp scissors, cut off a ¼ inch off the top the bag and about 1 inch off the bottom and then run the scissors along the seam of the bag to make one flat, square piece of material. Repeat for all the bags. ✪ Tape four bags together using duct tape or shiny aluminum electrical tape until you have a round of taped coffee bags.

Using an old piece of cardboard (like an old shipping box), measure the base of the coffee bag basket by placing the bag circle on top and tracing it with a pencil onto the cardboard. ✪ Cut out the round and use it as a template to make a circular piece of coffee bag material using the extra coffee bags and tape. ✪ Tape the circular piece to the bottom of the bag and finish it all off with clean strips of tape to give a clean, neat appearance on the outside.

LEGO CHESS SET

SUPPLIES: VARIETY OF STRAY LEGO PIECES (INCLUDING 1 LARGE BASEPLATE PIECE AND 32 SMALLER SQUARES) ✪ WOODEN SURFACE FOR BASE (OPTIONAL).

Even in an age of high tech video games, LEGOS continue to be one of the most popular toys with kids. With over 400 billion LEGO blocks created in the last five decades, you are likely to find storage bins and shoe boxes overflowing with stray LEGO pieces at any family home. And if you don't have children but would still like to give this upcycling project a try, don't run to the toy store: your local thrift shops are likely to have large plastic bags for sale at a fraction of the cost.

HOW TO: Start with the base: We used a 10 × 10-inch base and 32 contrasting 1¼-inch square base pieces to make the checkered base. If you don't have 32 matching square base pieces, you can always make them uniform in color by using a spray paint designed to work with plastic surfaces (available at any paint or hardware store).

You'll need contrasting sets for each side of the board: 1 king, 1 queen, 2 rooks, 2 bishops, 2 knights, and 8 pawns. You can design the pieces to be as fancy or as simple as possible, but make sure they are consistent in style and design for both colors.

If you want to strengthen the base of the game, you can also glue it to a wooden surface to make it sturdier or just rest it on top of a thick placemat (pictured here) when playing. Check, mate!

CHAPTER SIX:
SUMMER CELEBRATIONS

There's Memorial Day, the Fourth of July, and Labor Day. And while there are different reasons and meanings to these holidays, there are striking similarities to the way we celebrate them. They all involve being outdoors, a roaring grill, good food and drinks, and lots of family and friends. And maybe fireworks.

That's the reason I decided to dedicate this chapter simply to summer celebrations, because all of these holidays are very similar and share the basic premise of having the day off to basically party. But the ideas in this chapter aren't just designed for these three holidays; use them all summer long. For whatever reason you're having an outdoor fête (I've been known to have a tree-planting party; any excuse to get some manual labor done in exchange for free drinks), these helpful upcycling summery projects and tips will come in handy.

And if you're planning an outdoor wedding, there are lots of great ideas here, too.

SAND-GLITTERED LEAF PLACE MARKERS

SUPPLIES: LARGE LEAVES ✿ BEACH SAND ✿ WHITE CRAFT GLUE.

A few years ago, I was invited to a destination wedding at the balmy island of Anguilla. Upon arrival, I was met with a frantic message: The bride's handmade place markers she made herself in New York City had been tossed out from her honeymoon suite by housekeeping. It was my task—with a few hours before the wedding—to come up with a pretty and beautiful solution. Thinking like MacGyver, I scavenged the beach and collected 50 dried-up leaves, a bucket of sand (technically breaking my own eco-rule! See page 123), and a bottle of Elmer's glue that I took from the Kids Beach Camp summer room at the resort hotel.

And just like that, not only did I come up with a pretty solution for the stressed-out bride's big day, but I think created a wonderful upcycling project perfect for any celebratory event.

HOW TO: If you don't have access to dried, preserved leaves from a beach, collect leaves from the yard and press them between the pages of a heavy book. ✿ Let them press and dry out for a full week so they become flat and sturdy. ✿ Use white craft glue to spell out the guest's name onto the leaf; sprinkle white sand on top. ✿ Shake off the excess and allow to dry.

CONDIMENT CARRYING CASE

SUPPLIES: PAPER SIX-PACK CARRYING CASE ⊕ CONTACT PAPER ⊕ SCISSORS.

One thing that both vegetarians and carnivores can agree on when it comes to summer BBQ-ing is this: It's the condiments that can make or break a (veggie) burger or (soy) hot dog.

An easy way to carry kitchen condiments from indoors to outdoors is to reuse the six-pack carrying case that beer and soda often come in. But reusing a cardboard carrying case as is can be quite unsightly. But in just a few minutes, you can pretty one up so nobody will be any wiser that it once held six frosty brews.

HOW TO: Contact paper can be found in the kitchen supply section at any home-improvement stores like Lowe's. Choose a pattern that you like; one roll will be plenty to do several six-pack carrying cases. A paper six-pack case when empty will flatten easily, so push it flat to get started. ⊕ Place the flat case on top of the section of contact paper so the bottom of the case lays along the bottom edge of the contact paper, and cut out along the edges so it matches the shape of the case. ⊕ Repeat the back. ⊕ Trace the sides with a pencil on the contact paper, cut, and adhere to the sides. ⊕ Lay contact paper on the sides and use scissors to neatly cut it so it sits flush all around the edges. ⊕ Repeat until the entire container is covered.

STACKED ZEN ROCKS

SUPPLIES: RIVER ROCKS ✪ E-6000 GLUE ✪ PAINTER'S TAPE.

Every year, I make a trip to Tecate, Mexico, to spend a week at the wellness resort Rancho La Puerta. One of my favorite reasons for the annual trip is the 5 a.m. hikes up the mountain to see the sun rise and bask in the beautiful views. One thing I've noticed is that previous hikers have stacked rocks on top of each other in almost improbably Zen-like creations that are scattered here and there, going up and down the mountain. The towering stacks, which often remind me of the game of Jenga, seem like the formations should fall, but somehow they stay put for weeks if not months at a time.

This centerpiece idea is inspired by Rancho La Puerta, but with a little help from my favorite adhesive, E-6000. They take on the organic, almost-impossible look of stacked rocks, but will stay put no matter how hard anyone tries to knock them down.

HOW TO: Choose a variety of rocks and pebbles from a stream, river, or your own backyard. ✪ Scrub them clean and let them dry. ✪ Stack rocks on a table until you've reached a selection that looks natural and that balances on its own. ✪ Use E-6000 glue between each rock to attach them, and wrap painter's tape around to reinforce them. ✪ Allow them to dry for 24 hours, and remove the tape.

KOOL-AID-DYED TABLECLOTH

SUPPLIES: KOOL-AID PACKETS (NO SUGAR ADDED) ✪ SPRAY BOTTLE FULL OF WATER ✪ PAINTER'S TARP ✪ PLASTIC TRASH BAGS.

Think tie-dyeing, fruit-punch style. And if that isn't enough to make you curious, let me persuade you with this: This project is super cheap to make, and the end result looks deliciously luxe.

A word of warning: The Kool-Aid dye is so strong that not only will it dye fabric bright, vibrant colors, but getting it off your unprotected hands is quite the challenge. Be sure to protect your hands with super-thick rubber gloves to keep them rainbow-dyed free.

HOW TO: Launder a painter's tarp the size of your desired tablecloth; this will help soften the fabric and take out any creases from the fabric. ✪ Lay the painter's tarp on an outdoor table and cover the ground or table if you want to protect it from any dyeing; plastic trash bags work great and can be reused after the project. ✪ Start by spraying the edges of the cloth with water from a spray bottle; be liberal with the water to the point of almost totally soaking the tablecloth. ✪ While wearing gloves, sprinkle Kool-Aid in even stripes along the edges of the tablecloth so it sticks to the wet portions. ✪ Working in small sections at a time, once you've sprinkled the Kool-Aid, use the spray bottle to activate the Kool-Aid and keep spraying until it saturates the fabric and streaks. ✪ Add different colors until you achieve the desired design effect.

OVERSIZED UPCYCLED BIRD FEEDER

SUPPLIES: LARGE PLASTIC CONTAINER (LIKE A WAREHOUSE-CLUB-SIZE METHOD HAND-WASHING REFILL BOTTLE) ✛ X-ACTO KNIFE ✛ PLASTIC WASHERS ✛ CRAFT GLUE ✛ STONE ✛ TWINE ✛ BIRDSEED.

Several years ago, I worked with the home-cleaning company Method Products as a green consultant. I'd already been a longtime fan of the brand and used all of their products in my own home, so when the chance came up to work with them, I jumped. I was always impressed not only with their commitment to sustainability, but with their forward-thinking design with the packaging. Any company that can make laundry-detergent bottles look cool are A+ in my style book. It's their awesome packaging that inspired me to come up with this upcycling project.

If you don't have an oversized Method bottle, you can also use any oversized clear container for this project. Just be sure to use something that looks great and that you wouldn't be embarrassed to hang in your front yard for our feathered friends to feed from.

HOW TO: Clean and wash the bottle out thoroughly; make sure there isn't any residue whatsoever inside, so it won't make birds sick. ✛ Once dry, cut out two holes—one in the front and one in the back—using an X-Acto knife. ✛ Insert a plastic washer in the hole; this will create a smooth edge so the just-cut plastic hole isn't razor-sharp when birds poke their heads through to feed. ✛ Fill feeder with birdseed ✛ Glue a stone at the top of the bottle so water won't seep inside. ✛ Tie a piece of twine tightly around the neck of the bottle and hang the bird feeder from a tree. ✛ Place a branch through both holes so the birds have a place to rest.

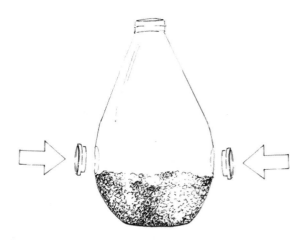

PLASTIC SEA-URCHIN CENTERPIECE

SUPPLIES: PLASTIC WATER BOTTLES ✪ SCISSORS ✪ FLOWERS.

I know some of you think there's no point in making your own centerpieces since you can buy beautiful arrangements at any florist these days, but this simply isn't true. First of all, those centerpieces are pretty to look at, but are usually very expensive to buy. And one large centerpiece with a cluster of flowers looks just like that: a bunch of store-bought flowers you stuck into a generic vase in the middle of the table.

To be a bit more creative and to save loads of money, try this plastic sea-urchin centerpiece idea. You'll need several clear plastic water bottles to make this, so raid the trash bin at your office or gym to get bottles if you don't have any. And then grab a dozen inexpensive flowers in a bunch from the supermarket or your own yard to finish off this project. These cheap flowers—we're talking carnations here—will look almost ethereal floating inside each plastic sea urchin.

HOW TO: Cut a plastic water bottle in half. ✪ Using sharp scissors, cut thin strips from the top of the cut bottle down about 1 to 2 inches all around. ✪ Use your fingers to "fuss" the strips until they are twisted, bent and not perfectly neat. ✪ Fill the bottle with water and float a flower inside.

THREE QUICK AND EASY UPCYCLING IDEAS

SUPPLIES: BANDANAS ✪ PAINT CHIPS ✪ SCISSORS ✪ GLASS JARS ✪ A HOLE PUNCH ✪ STRAWS.

Here are three quick and easy upcycling ideas you can use for your next summertime bash.

The first one is something I do all the time and love because it's eco-friendly and dirt cheap. I buy cotton bandanas from my outdoor sporting goods store (choose whatever colors you love) and use them in place of disposable napkins. I find with bandanas that guests feel less guilty wiping their BBQ-stained mouths with them because they aren't the starch-white antique napkins you often associate with cloth napkins. Bandanas are a great eco-friendly alternative because they are cheap, machine-washable, and often come in dark, stain-hiding colors.

The second idea involves oversized paint chips. Simply cut them into squares or circles large enough to cover a glass (or, as pictured, upcycled jars) and punch a hole in the middle of the paint chip. Insert a straw through the hole. You've got instant drink covers that will keep pesky bugs from flying into drinks and guests can keep track of their drinks based on the color of the paint-chip cover.

The third idea has some festive alliteration: Jam-Jelly Juice Jars. Saying it five times fast will definitely be more difficult than actually executing the idea. All you need to do start is to indulge in some delicious jams and jellies. Save the jars and lids and clean then really well with hot, soapy water. For your next picnic, fill them with fresh juices, screw on the lid, and you've got a portable leak-proof drinking container. This is a perfect thing to use for kids' parties, or make them grown-up with a shot of liquor to the juice. Cheers!

CLOCKWISE FROM TOP LEFT:

COTTON BANDANA NAPKINS, PAINT-CHIP DRINK COVERS,

JAM-JELLY JARS

UPCYCLED FABRIC CHAIN-LINK GARLAND

SUPPLIES: T-SHIRTS OR OLD JEANS ✛ SHARP SCISSORS ✛ BINDER CLIPS ✛ TWINE.

There's just something about a garland that says "party" to me because of its free form: It swoops up and down either from the wooden beams up on the ceiling, from around the edge of a buffet table, or above a roaring fireplace. Whatever time it is, a seasonal garland can turn a casual get-together into a full-on party.

This project is what I call my Great Goodwill Project because it uses old and unwearable T-shirts and jeans. Be sure to choose colorful fabric that is suitable for your party. For the Fourth of July, look for red, white, and blue fabric. For Christmas, think green and red. Halloween? Yep, you guessed it: orange and black.

HOW TO: Cut two strips of fabric approximately 20 to 24 inches long with a 3-inch diameter. ✛ Roll both pieces into a thinner strip and braid them together, using binder clips as you go along to secure the braid. ✛ Use a piece of twine to tie the finished braid into a circle, and remove the clips. ✛ Repeat, and add braided links as you go along to make your garland.

WOODEN SHIPPING-
PALLET BAR

SUPPLIES: WOODEN SHIPPING PALLETS ○ PAINT ○ BRUSH.

What would a summer celebration be without a bar?

This upcycling project is big on storage, dramatic on appearances, and a cinch to make. The hardest part? Trying to find a local retailer who is willing to part with a stack of wooden packing pallets.

The good news is that it's not too hard to find someone willing to give them to you. In case you are wondering what a wooden pallet is, they are used to load and unload merchandise to stores; the open parts between the top and bottom are where forklifts pick up the pallet, to move everything from potting soil to farm equipment from the truck to the store. My advice to you to find these is to just be friendly with a store manager at a major store that has tons of these pallets, and you'll be surprised how easy it is to get these for this project.

Once you get your hands on about eight packing pallets, all you need to do is paint them a color you like. This is a great way to use up leftover house paint. Then stack them up and use the empty spaces to store bottles of wine, water, and soda and anything else you need to entertain like a pro all summer long.

All throughout the backyard of my house in Bucks County, Pennsylvania, are groves of young bamboo plants that were planted way before I ever bought the house. How they got there is anybody's guess, but the mini panda's buffet exists and I use it for all sorts of decorating throughout the year, including this American Pride project.

This project is inspired by that grove, and I love how it marries Asian design influence (the bamboo) with Spirit Pride (the flags), much like yours truly is as a Korean American lifestyle authority.

FOURTH OF JULY BAMBOO POLES

SUPPLIES: BAMBOO STALKS ✪ WHITE CRAFT GLUE ✪ SMALL AMERICAN FLAGS ON WOODEN STAKES ✪ TERRA COTTA POTS AND SAND (OPTIONAL).

HOW TO: To make this, all you need to do is cut bamboo stalks in approximately 3-foot lengths, squeeze some glue inside the bamboo pole, and stick an American flag inside. ✪ Let it dry and decorate away. ✪ Either stick the bamboo flags into the ground or fill terra cotta pots with sand (as pictured here) and decorate the table with flags.

TREE STUMP CHAIRS

SUPPLIES: TREE STUMPS ✪ PAINTER'S TAPE ✪ VALSPAR GLOSS SPRAY PAINT ✪ THUMBTACKS ✪ RUBBER MALLET ✪ SANDPAPER ✪ BANDANA (OPTIONAL).

If a tree falls in the woods, does it make a sound? I have no idea, but I do know that I would turn the stump into a chair for my party.

I should admit that when I made this project, I didn't wait for a tree to come to its demise in my own backyard. Instead, I visited a local lumberyard where certain stumps were discarded for not being worthy of being made into lumber. These discarded pieces were sold to me for $5 and I found them perfect for seating.

To find stumps, you can call local arborists or tree-service companies and ask them to save you pieces from their next job. It's surprisingly easy and you'll get some great pieces to upcycle. Don't have green guilt about getting these stumps: Often trees fall due to age or a ravaging storm, so they had to be cut up anyway.

HOW TO: To make glossy stripes, use painter's tape to block off any section you don't want painted with spray paint; work in sections at a time, and paint away. The gold stars on one of the stumps were simply made by drawing out a star using a pencil; it was filled in with golden thumbtacks that were gently tapped into the wood using a rubber mallet.

✪ Use sandpaper to make the top of the stump smooth, and cover with a bandana if desired.

TEA-TIN CARRYING CASE

SUPPLIES: VARIETY OF 6 TEA TINS ✚ METAL HANDLE ✚ WOODEN SCREWS ✚ CORDLESS SCREWDRIVER ✚ PIECE OF WOOD.

Tea lovers, listen: Those decorative tea tins you've been hoarding in your pantry even though they don't hold any tea can now have a functional use.

While pretty Chinese and English tins look the most attractive for this upcycling project, you don't need to resort to being an aesthetic snob when drinking tea. Drink what you love, but save tins that look best and recycle the rest in your curbside recycling bin.

Use the tea-tin carrying case for all sorts of parties: carry utensils, napkins, straws, and anything else that fits inside to make kitchen accessories a little bit easier to bring outdoors. In the summer months, keep it stocked with your regular essentials and have it ready at any given time to entertain outdoors.

HOW TO: Line up six tea tins—three in the front and three in the back—in a desired row so they are as close to even in length on both sides as possible. ✚ Cut a piece of wood (I used one that was 1½ inches square) that is the length of the finished tea-tin carrying tray. ✚ Using the cordless screwdriver, drill a wooden screw through a tea tin into the wood, securing it into place. ✚ Repeat until all the tea tins are attached. ✚ Screw in a handle on top of the wood strip.

One battle that many of us face during the summer months is with biting, flying, whirring mosquitoes that can turn any outdoor party into a war zone. Many people resort to using toxic sprays, others prefer unusual techniques like turning on fans to blow the biting bugs away. I like to use a more natural remedy for the situation, and find that burning citronella candles can be an effective way to keep them at bay.

CITRONELLA LOCKET

SUPPLIES: LOCKET NECKLACE WITH CHAIN ✚ CITRONELLA CANDLE.

One way to make a personal mosquito repellant that's both effective and stylish is to wear this citronella locket. It looks way more complicated than it really is: Start with a vintage locket (this is from a flea market) and clean it well with a damp cloth. Then light a citronella candle and pour the melted wax into the well of the locket. Allow to cool and wear!

UPCYCLING IDEA
FOR CHILLING BEVERAGES

On a hot summer day, there is nothing more refreshing than an almost bone-chilling soda, bottle of water, or frosty beer.

While a refrigerator will surely do the trick, that option is a luxurious rarity for most of us to have outdoors.

My two favorite ideas to keep beverages cold involve what's already outdoors. One idea is to take a wheelbarrow and transform it into a chilling station. Start by filling it with old bubble wrap; it'll help cushion the bottles so they don't shatter, and fill up space so you don't have to buy a dozen bags of ice to fill the wheelbarrow up. Place bottles on top of the bubble wrap, open a few bags of ice, and scatter the cubes around to get everything ice cold. When the ice melts, just tip the wheelbarrow onto your plants to give them a nice drink.

The other idea is perfect if you're near a stream at your party. Just place bottles in a bubbly creek and let the cold water keep them cold. Whenever guests need a drink, they can roll up their pants and enjoy a cool soak, all while getting their refreshing beverage. Just remember to remove empty or unopened bottles from the creek after the party.

CHAPTER SEVEN:
SPOOKY HALLOWEEN

I live on a haunted road. When I moved into my current home several years ago, I was met by a kind neighbor who gave me what I could only call a mostly nice gift basket. I say mostly nice because in addition to a bottle of local wine, homemade peanut brittle, and a greeting card, it also contained a book about the haunted roads of Bucks County, Pennsylvania. Inside the book was a chapter about my very own road and the supposed spirits and ghosts that haunt it. While I've never seen ghosts myself, even the rumor of spirits is enough for me to embrace Halloween a wee bit more in my new home.

Scary stories aside, I do take Halloween seriously at my home. It's really the perfect backdrop: black painted house, deep in the woods, surrounded by orange-blazing trees in the October month. Spooky decorations, well, just pop, and kids who are brave enough to trek up the dark and scary driveway to my home are rewarded with what I call "super treats." You know those giant oversized candy bars you

think you've only seen in *Willy Wonka & the Chocolate Factory*? Yes, that's what we're talking about when I say super treats.

However you celebrate Halloween, there are hauntingly boo-tiful ideas in this chapter. While I don't pick favorite chapters, this one surely is up there as one of the best, and I hope it will inspire you to get your home All Hallows' Eve ready, whether you have ghosts on your street or not.

SHOPPING-BAG CHALKBOARD SILHOUETTE TREE

SUPPLIES: SEVERAL PAPER GROCERY-STORE BAGS ✛ PAINTER'S TAPE ✛ BLACK CHALKBOARD PAINT ✛ FOAM BRUSHES ✛ DOUBLE-STICK TAPE ✛ SCISSORS ✛ CHALK.

I seem to always have a stash of brown-paper grocery store bags in my kitchen cabinets. The paper bags somehow end up here, whether it's my own fault for failing to bring reusable bags when I make a last-minute run for snacks or someone visits and leaves it behind for me to reuse. For whatever reason, there's no need to feel bad about having a few of these disposable paper bags since they can also be a great material to upcycle during the spooky Halloween season.

Don't feel like you are limited to just the silhouette tree design. Feel free to cut out any Halloween shape you see fit for your home: ghosts, headstones, a witch, or a patch of pumpkins would look amazing, too.

HOW TO: Rip open three or four brown-paper grocery store bags until they are flat pieces of paper. ✛ Tape them together on one side using painter's tape so you have one, large flat surface of material to work with. ✛ On the opposite side, paint several coats of black chalkboard paint, doing light layers and allowing each layer to dry before applying another coat. ✛ Once dry, use chalk to trace out the silhouette shape you want, then cut it out using sharp scissors. ✛ Use double-stick tape to attach your silhouette to a window and add detail to it using chalk.

UPCYCLED FLOODLIGHT "POTION" BOTTLES

SUPPLIES: BURNT-OUT FLOODLIGHTS ✛ WINE CORKS ✛ BLACK ELECTRICAL TAPE ✛ BLACK CRAFT PAINT ✛ FINE-TIP BRUSH.

This project was really the whole inspiration for *Upcycled Celebrations* for two reasons: It uses something that is truly trash (the burnt-out bulb) and it transforms it into something charmingly perfect for Halloween in two supereasy steps. When I made these for a Halloween party one year, even my most craft-challenged friends thought they were cute and easy for them to create!

The key thing here is to remember this: Don't run to the home-improvement store and buy new floodlights. It defeats the purpose. But if you must, you can make these potion bottles first with new bulbs and come November 1, wipe off the paint, strip off the tape, and use the bulbs for their intended purpose.

HOW TO: The simplicity of this tutorial is ridiculously easy: Attach a wine cork to the socket using black electrical tape. ✛ Write a spooky message like "Poison" or "Beware!" onto the bulb using black craft paint. ✛ Display.

TOY-ANIMAL STAG HEADS

SUPPLIES: OLD CHILDREN'S TOYS ✪ UNFINISHED WOOD PLAQUES ✪ SCISSORS ✪ E-6000 GLUE OR HOT GLUE ✪ BLACK CRAFT PAINT ✪ BRUSH.

If there are kids in the room, you may want to ask them to leave before reading on about this upcycling project. The reason? You might be tempted to do something rather morbid with their toys.

Yes, this project calls for decapitating toys for their heads. But it's all in good fun and frankly, it's much more humane than actual animals being hunted and mounted for display. And especially if the toy in question is no longer being played with, why not have a little fun and create a stag-head collection of toy store curiosities?

If you don't have any toy animals to terrorize, your local thrift store will have a treasure trove of animals, dolls, dinosaurs, robots, and more.

HOW TO: Paint the unfinished wood plaques (from Michaels stores) with a coat or two of black craft paint. ✪ Allow to dry completely. ✪ With sharp scissors, cut off the head of whatever you want to mount. ✪ Run a strip of hot glue or E-6000 adhesive (which is stronger, depending on the weight of whatever you're mounting) along the cut portion of the head. ✪ Press it against the front of the plaque and allow to dry. ✪ Hang on wall using 3M Command mounting strips or strong double-stick tape.

SPOOKY-GHOST BOTTLE CANDLEHOLDERS

SUPPLIES: GLASS WINE OR SODA BOTTLES ⊕ BLACK AND WHITE SPRAY MATTE PAINT (I USED VALSPAR BRAND, AVAILABLE AT LOWE'S STORES) ⊕ WHITE TAPER CANDLES.

I admit that this project is deceptively simplistic-looking to make, but is not. Let me explain: It all depends on your skill level with a bottle of spray paint. If your trigger finger is like a lead foot on a brake, you may want to practice finessing with a bottle of paint before you ruin a pile of glass recyclables.

But once you get a feel for how paint dispenses from your bottle of spray paint, this upcycling project takes just a few minutes to make a whole collection of candleholders. Don't fret if the black paint drips a teeny bit when you apply the ghost faces; it just makes it more charming in the end result.

HOW TO: Apply two light coats of white spray paint to the outside of the glass bottles and allow to dry; about 30 minutes on a dry day should do. ⊕ Then hold on to the can of black spray paint and apply two eyes and a mouth, spraying close to the bottle and doing it rather quickly. ⊕ Stick a white taper candle into the top of the bottle and light.

UPCYCLED BONES

SUPPLIES: NEWSPAPER ✪ MASKING TAPE ✪ PLASTER GAUZE STRIPS (AVAILABLE AT MICHAELS STORES) ✪ BOWL OF WATER.

If I had to choose just one project from this Halloween chapter for you to try, this is the one. It's totally foolproof, cheap to make, and the finished item—if I do say so myself—is awesome. Who wouldn't want to fill a bowl with Flintstone-esque bones on Halloween? If you've got kids, this is also a great project to get them involved in because instead of writing advice like "and this step is where the parents should do it," I don't have to. It's all kid-friendly from start to finish.

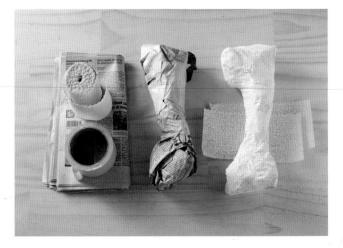

HOW TO: Crumple several sheets of newspaper into the shape of a bone by rolling, twisting, and bending it into crumpled logs; use masking tape around the center to help form the bone shape. ✪ Dip strips of the plaster gauze in water and wrap it around the newspaper until the whole thing is covered. ✪ Allow to dry overnight.

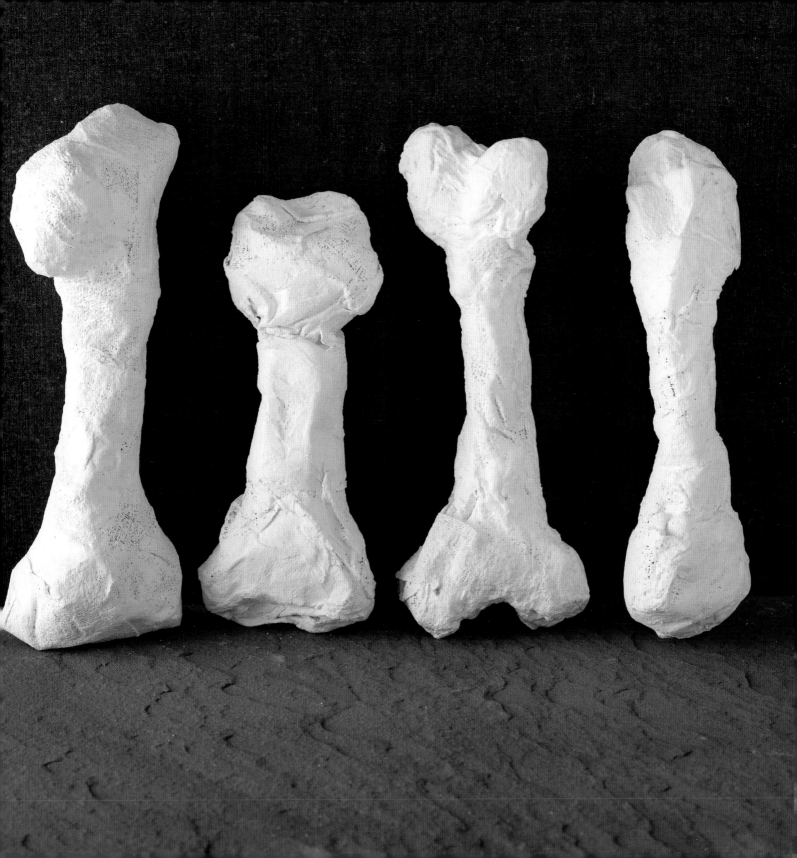

If you have a globe in the attic that still has the words "Union of Soviet Socialist Republic" on it, it may be time to upcycle it into something a bit more current.

One Halloween, I decided to go the nontraditional route and pick up delicious candies that are sold all over the world from my local specialty-food stores. Now, before you think this also means kids are going to trick my house out of disappointment, I will say in my defense they are always excited to try a new candy that is different from the standard chocolate-covered nougat bars my neighbors give.

GLOBAL-TREAT BOWLS

SUPPLIES: OLD CARDBOARD GLOBE ✚ BLUNT BUTTER KNIFE.

To play up the global-treat theme, I like to use these global-treat bowls upcycled from old globes and they are very simple to make. Just use a blunt knife (like a butter knife) to pry open the globe at the equator. Unscrew the hardware inside the globe that holds it to the stand and voilà! You've got two bowls.

WINE BOTTLE CANDLES

SUPPLIES: GLASS WINE BOTTLES ⊕ COTTON CANDLEWICK STRING (FROM MICHAELS CRAFT STORES) ⊕ METAL BOLT ⊕ OLD CANDLES ⊕ CRAYONS (OPTIONAL) ⊕ BUCKET ⊕ OLD SAUCEPANS ⊕ HAMMER ⊕ OLD TOWEL ⊕ DRY BRUSH.

I came across this idea one evening over a bottles of wine and a flickering candle at the Italian restaurant Gemma in New York City. In my slightly inebriated state (which I will admit is when I come up with my weirdest upcycling ideas), I saw the flicker of the candle above the wine bottle and wondered why can't the glass bottle be a mold to make a wine-bottle shaped candle? Just pour melted wax in, insert wick, chill, crash bottle, and *voilà!* Wine-shaped candle!

Well, thirty attempts later, I had success, and you can avoid my mistakes if you follow my instructions carefully. And my advice to those of you who think you can use your good cookware to melt candles for this project: Don't. No matter how precise and clean you think you'll be, wax will drip inside and outside your pots and pans, making them almost useless the next time you want to cook actual food. So, use whatever you've been planning to toss out.

HOW TO: Use a hammer to break up old candles and place the wax (minus their old wicks) inside a smaller saucepan. ⊕ Estimate how much wax you'll need based on the size of the wine bottle and number of finished candles you want to make. You can break up old crayons to dye the wax too, if you wish. ⊕ Boil some water in the larger saucepan and place the smaller one inside that is full of wax chips; simmer it until melted and lower the temperature to keep it that way. ⊕ Tie a wick around a small metal bolt that can fit inside the mouth of the bottle, and drop it inside. ⊕ Tie the wick around the neck of the bottle. ⊕ Pour the melted wax halfway up the bottle and immediately place it into a bucket full of ice-cold water. ⊕ Fifteen minutes later, add more wax until it's three-quarters full, and plunge again. ⊕ Fifteen minutes later, add more wax to the top of the bottle, and plunge. ⊕ Examine the top of the bottle and add more wax until it has solidified completely to the top. ⊕ Chill for another two hours and add ice or new cold water to the bucket if it gets lukewarm. ⊕ The chilling process helps settle and harden the wax and gives the finished candle a shiny, solid sheen.

Place the glass wine bottle inside large towels and fold over it so it's completely covered. ⊕ Using a hammer, carefully smash the glass while it's covered. ⊕ Shake the glass off the bottle (and use a dry brush to remove any small shards) to reveal your finished candle.

UPCYCLED TRICK-OR-TREAT BAG

SUPPLIES: PAPER SHOPPING BAG ⊕ CHALKBOARD PAINT ⊕ BRUSH ⊕ CHALK ⊕ DECORATIVE TOP (OPTIONAL).

This project didn't start off with any intended purpose. In fact, I just happened to have a sturdy paper bag from a shopping trip to Ralph Lauren and saw a can of used black chalkboard paint and just went along with my upcycling instincts. The finished result, I thought, was not only an adorable alternative to the ubiquitous plastic pumpkin trick-or-treat totes you see on Halloween, but better: You can customize it on front with a unique message or quotation, with chalk.

Use whatever paper bag you want here, but splurge on one of the sturdier shopping bags from a nice store instead of a paper grocery-store bag for this project. If my memory serves me correctly, Halloween isn't just about trick or treating, it's also about hoarding sugary sweets. You want this bag to hold plenty of treats all night long without it ripping and having candy strewn all over the street.

HOW TO: Paint the entire outside of the bag with several coats of chalkboard paint. If you want, you can cut the existing handles and thread rope in its place to make a more decorative handle. ⊕ Use chalk to decorate the front with whatever drawing or saying you want.

TOMBSTONE TREAT BOXES

SUPPLIES: OLD FEDEX OR UPS BOXES ✛ MASKING TAPE ✛ VALSPAR FAUX "STONE"-FINISH SPRAY PAINT ✛ CRAFT-STORE LETTERS ✛ SCISSORS ✛ HOLE PUNCH ✛ TWINE.

Kids are picky, so I'm offering another option for hauling their Halloween treats around the neighborhood. It involves using a used FedEx or UPS box, a little spray paint, and some basic decorating skills.

Don't go to your local shipping place and use a brand-new shipping box for this project. Instead, ask your friend who receives a lot of overnight mail for work or save a box the next time you get a special delivery. Give yourself about 24 hours to make this project since the paint needs time to properly set. If you try to rush this on October 31, your little tyke may end up with bits of stone spray paint on their costume. And that would not be ghostly, but ghastly.

HOW TO: Make sure one end of the box is securely closed; if not, add a little masking tape. ✛ Use scissors to cut the open side into the silhouette of a tombstone. ✛ Spray paint the whole thing using the faux stone-finish spray paint; you may need several coats to achieve the desired effect and to fully conceal the graphics on the box. ✛ Once dry, use a hole punch to cut out two holes on the side and thread some twine through as a handle. ✛ Decorate with letters or Halloween silhouette stickers from the craft store if desired.

While upcycling by definition is a very eco-friendly activity because it transforms trash into something new, I particularly love this project because it incorporates items you may be throwing away along with the latest in eco-friendly technology. It's a great example of upcycling and gets bonus points for being even more eco-conscious, too.

It only works with outdoor solar lanterns because solar lights use internal rechargeable batteries to power up internal LED bulbs at night. If we used hard-wired lights, you'd have to deal with cords, electrical wiring and all sorts of aesthetic headaches to make this work. So, solar just makes sense.

SPOOKY SOLAR GHOSTS

SUPPLIES: SOLAR LANTERNS ✪ OLD WHITE SHEETS ✪ BLACK CRAFT PAPER ✪ SCISSORS ✪ DOUBLE-STICK TAPE ✪ STRING.

HOW TO: Start by finding the center of the bed sheet (I used twin-size sheets) and cut a hole using scissors. ✪ Drape it over the solar light and have the top of the light hook come through the sheet. ✪ Hang it using string or rope from a tree. ✪ Add two eyes with black craft paper and tape and wait for the sun to go down. Illuminated ghosts . . . so pretty.

SHRUNKEN APPLE HEADS

SUPPLIES: APPLES ✚ PEELER OR SMALL KNIFE ✚ SALT ✚ BAKING SHEET ✚ LEMON JUICE ✚ BLACK PEPPERCORNS.

Think vegan head-shrinking here. Or just a clever way to use apples that are a bit past their prime.

All of my New York City friends have a weird fascination with coming to my home in Bucks County, Pennsylvania, and going apple picking. As someone who has lived on a farm, I guess I have a hard time understanding the charm of spending my free time picking apples. But I humor them, and I end up with a bumper crop of unwanted apples from their day at the orchard.

This upcycling project is the result of apple overload. I can't decide whether to blame or thank my friends who ironically come from the Big Apple for this project, but here is this adorably cute upcycling idea.

HOW TO: Start by peeling all of the skin off the apple using a vegetable peeler or small knife, depending on your skill level. ✚ Carve a face including an extra large nose, indentations for the mouth and eyes, and anything else you want to personalize your apple guy (or gal). ✚ Squirt some lemon juice all over the outside. ✚ Sprinkle salt onto a baking sheet and place the apple on top (the salt will prevent the apple from sticking and help draw out moisture). ✚ Bake at 180°F overnight or for 24 hours, to slowly dry it out. ✚ Use peppercorns for the eyes.

BAT DOG COSTUME

SUPPLIES: USED CARDBOARD BOX ✛ BLACK CHALKBOARD PAINT ✛ BRUSH ✛ CHALK ✛ THIN RIBBON ✛ SCISSORS.

Dog costumes are tricky. Tricky, because it's not really what our imagination conjures up for what our canine companions can become on Halloween, but really what they are in the mood to tolerate. When coming up with costumes for this book, I tested a few that included masks, head gear, and body suits. Every dog—from a small-as-can-be Chihuahua all the way up to a giant Great Dane—rejected anything that obstructed their view or felt like it constricted their ability to run and walk. So, the cardboard bat wings were born.

What I love about this upcycling project is that it's fairly simple to make and it can be tailored to fit any size dog; you can make giant bat wings for an extra-large dog or make tiny ones for a pocket-size pooch. And it's very inexpensive to create. So, if the dog happens to Houdini himself out of the bat costume later in the night, there will be no anger in losing some old cardboard wings.

HOW TO: Find a piece of flattened cardboard and trace out a set of bat wings using a pencil. The wings should be size appropriate for the size of the dog wearing them. ✛ Cut out the wings with scissors and paint the front and back with two coats of black chalkboard paint.

Once dry, poke two holes at the top of the wings using one of the scissor blades and run one piece of grosgrain ribbon through both holes and then tie it around the neck of the dog so it's taut, but not constricting to the dog. ✛ Embellish the wings with veins using chalk.

BUTTERFLY WINGS

SUPPLIES: USED CARDBOARD BOX ✪ VARIETY OF CRAFT PAINTS ✪ BRUSH ✪ POM-POMS ✪ GLITTER ✪ SCISSORS ✪ RIBBON ✪ WIRE ✪ HEADBAND (OPTIONAL).

What I adore about this upcycling project is that you can make it with your child who wants to be a beautiful butterfly for Halloween. And because there's no right or wrong way to make it, the end result will be absolutely beautiful. They can squeeze, plop, and brush on as much paint on one side of the cardboard butterfly wings and when you fold over the unpainted half, you have a true masterpiece.

HOW TO: Depending on the size of your child, cut butterfly wings out of an old cardboard box that looks best on them; they can be dainty or extra-large. There really is no right or wrong size here.

Fold the wings in half down the middle and then unfold them so they lay flat. ✪ Using a number of craft paints, liberally apply paint to one half of the wings in whatever pattern you want to do. Be fast, since the paint can dry quickly, and then fold over the unpainted half on top to transfer the excess paint and create a matching pattern. ✪ Glue on poms-poms or sprinkle glitter to add extra flair to the wings and allow the whole thing to dry.

Cut two holes at the top of the wings and two holes at the bottom and thread a piece of grosgrain ribbon through the left side and right side to create straps; attach and knot into place so they are snug on the body. Optional: Add wire to a headband and glue poms-poms on top to play up the butterfly theme.

POPCORN BOY COSTUME

SUPPLIES: USED CARDBOARD BOX ✪ JAR OR CUP ✪ RED AND WHITE CRAFT PAINT ✪ BRUSH ✪ RIBBON ✪ BRADS ✪ SCISSORS ✪ STYROFOAM PACKING PEANUTS ✪ OLD PIECE OF FABRIC OR TRASH BAG ✪ YELLOW SPRAY PAINT ✪ HEAVY NEEDLE ✪ THREAD ✪ WIRE (OPTIONAL) ✪ BASEBALL CAP (OPTIONAL).

There used to be two choices when it came to kids' costumes: Go to one of those mysterious Halloween stores that seem to pop up in abandoned storefronts and get an expensive PVC costume in a bag, or sew some elaborate wardrobe together that only a Tony Award–winning costumer could whip up.

In my view of upcycling, a Halloween costume should be fun, make sense, use what you have, and involve a modicum of skill to pull off. This charming Popcorn Boy costume I think does the trick.

HOW TO: Find a large cardboard box that is big enough to fit around the torso of the child, but not so large it is cumbersome. ✪ Cut off the top and bottom panels so you are left with an open cube. ✪ On the top edge cut a scallop pattern using a jar or cup as a stencil. ✪ Using red craft paint, paint stripes of red (and add white stripes if you really want to make it look like a popcorn box) on the outside of the box. ✪ Set aside to dry.

With your pile of old Styrofoam packing peanuts, place them on top of an old piece of fabric or trash bag and lightly dust them with a few strokes of yellow spray paint; there is no need to saturate the packing peanuts with paint since you are trying to replicate the light butter topping found on movie theater popcorn. ✪ Once dry, thread the packing peanuts onto a long string of durable thread. It's up to you how much popcorn you want to make to fill the box.

Add two brads in the front of the box and two brads in the back, and thread ribbon to the box so they work as suspenders; knot the ribbon so it's comfortable and can hang on its own on the child. ✪ String the garlands of packing peanuts around the child and inside the box, hanging some on the outside. ✪ For an added touch, you can also attach some packing peanuts to wire and have them sticking out of the holes of a colorful baseball cap.

ANGRY-AS-HELL MASK

SUPPLIES: CEREAL BOX ✪ SCISSORS ✪ X-ACTO KNIFE ✪ BLACK PAINT ✪ BRUSH ✪ HOLE PUNCH ✪ FLORIST WIRE ✪ OLD POLYESTER PILLOW ✪ HOT-GLUE GUN.

I lived in the West Village in New York City for many years, and one of the annual traditions that brought thousands of people to my neck of the woods was the Halloween parade. And as much as I loved the parade and enjoy the debauchery as much as everyone else, I don't see the payoff in spending days (if not weeks) in crafting a costume to wear for a few hours on October 31. I like the idea of costumes and I like the idea of a DIY outfit, but I don't like the idea of spending that much time making something for one night of fun.

So, this mask is my solution to it all: it's clever, it's impactful, and when you're ready to go back to being normal, all you have to do is take it off.

HOW TO: Use the front of a cereal box and cut out a mask that fits your face; cut out the eyes using scissors or an X-Acto knife. If the first attempt doesn't seem right, don't worry! You still have the back of the cereal box for a second shot. ✪ Paint the finished mask with black paint and allow to dry. ✪ Punch two holes on the left and right of the mask and run a strip of florist wire so it fits snugly around your own head when you put the mask on. ✪ Cut two long strips of florist wire (approximately 20 inches long) and twist them onto the wire at each side at a place so it appears they are coming out of your ears when you wear the mask. ✪ Using hot glue, use the filling from the inside of an old polyester pillow to make the "steam," twisting and gluing the filling onto the wire and into a giant "poof" at the end. ✪ Feel free to have creative license here to make it as "angry" as you want.

CHAPTER EIGHT:
THANKSGIVING

As a vegetarian, cooking an entire traditional Thanksgiving meal from scratch isn't all that appealing; specifically, roasting a dead bird in the oven all morning long. And forget about "treating" my family to a hearty, delicious plant-based feast; they will have none of that since they are all die-hard carnivores. So for the past few years I had compromised: I have booked hotel rooms outside Washington, D.C., where we usually check in, drink wine all day, and let the hotel's restaurant appease our finicky palettes. The hotel is connected to a shopping mall, so on Black Friday, we nurse our hangovers with retail therapy and Bloody Marys.

After doing this for several years, I finally came to the conclusion that this wasn't really a tradition. After all, I entertain for a living—I should have a proper feast in my home. So this past year I put an end to our hotel Thanksgivings by stopping—pardon the pun—cold turkey

There's just one thing: I cannot bring myself to unwrap a Butterball and pretend the carcass does not offend me. So for our first home Thanksgiving, a local caterer fixed turkey and gravy and delivered it to my doorstep in the morning. I made the rest: roasted vegetables, stuffing, mashed potatoes, fresh cranberry sauce, rolls, and a sweet dessert. And since upcycling is the only way of entertaining I know, I decorated the table and house with a lot of fun ideas. I hope they will help you welcome family and friends into your own home.

Look, I know there's never a real situation where you're bringing a bottle of wine to a party and are perplexed on how to carry it. For most of us, we grab the neck of the bottle, swing it into a bag or the front seat of the car, and off we go. But this is Thanksgiving after all, and a bottle of red can be a bit more welcoming with some presentation panache. And with this upcycling project, the carrier is handsome enough to sit beautifully on the table or home bar. P.S.: When it's not carrying wine, you can also carry a reusable water bottle inside, swing it onto your shoulder, and off you go with a stylish hydration-to-go.

BELTED WINE-CARRYING CASE

SUPPLIES: NATURAL ROPE ✚ HOT-GLUE GUN ✚ LEATHER BELT.

HOW TO: Be sure your hot-glue gun is good and ready by plugging it in about 20 minutes before you start the project. Have plenty of glue sticks on hand, too. ✚ Start with the base of the carrier by coiling rope and gluing as you go along. ✚ When your circle of rope is slightly larger than the bottle of wine, start building it up along the sides, gluing as you coil. ✚ Glue a leather belt to the bottom and sides and allow to dry completely before using.

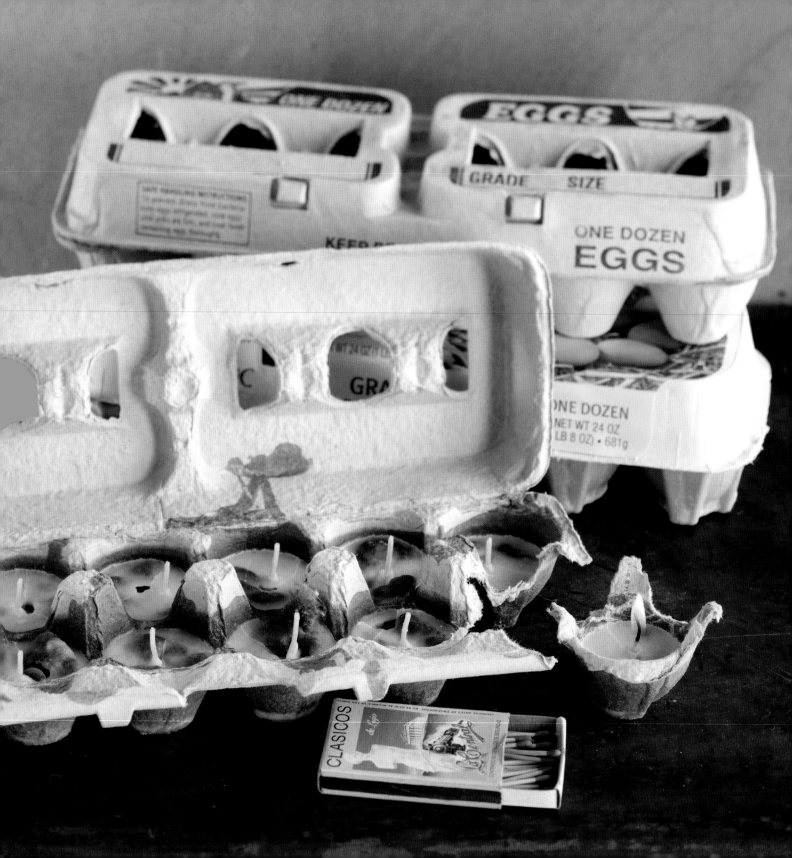

If rubbing two sticks together doesn't do the trick, here's a warm welcome gift to get the fire roaring in the fireplace, backyard fire pit, or BBQ grill. Save up lots of cardboard egg cartons before you make this project; why make just one fire-starter gift when you can upcycle a bunch to have ready to go? By the way, you can beef up the gift by adding a bundle of wood, some kindling, new matches, and maybe a bag of marshmallows to give the ultimate house "warming" gift.

EGG-CARTON FIRE STARTERS

SUPPLIES: CARDBOARD EGG CARTONS ✪ OLD CANDLES ✪ OLD SAUCEPAN AND LARGER POT ✪ WICKS FROM THE CRAFT STORE ✪ DRYER LINT.

HOW TO: Break up some old candles and place them inside an old saucepan; place that pot inside a larger pot with about an inch of water and simmer until the wax is melted. ✪ Shred small pieces of dryer lint and place them inside each compartment in the egg carton. ✪ Pour hot wax into each compartment. ✪ When the wax is cooling, but still warm, insert a 1-inch wick in the middle of each one. To use, just tear an egg-carton compartment out, light, and place wherever you want the fire to roar.

GOLD-LEAF WISHBONES

SUPPLIES: WISHBONES ✪ GOLD-LEAFING PEN (I USE KRYLON BRAND AVAILABLE AT MICHAELS) ✪ HYDROGEN PEROXIDE ✪ CONTAINER WITH LID ✪ SMALL HANGTAG (OPTIONAL) ✪ MINI ALPHABET STAMP SET AND INKPAD (OPTIONAL).

I know what you might be thinking: The vegetarian upcycling author has just come up with an idea using animal bones in a project. He won't eat the turkey, but he'll gladly craft with its bones. Let me explain.

First, let me say that I do not eat turkey on Thanksgiving and haven't for over 20 years. But that doesn't mean I can't appreciate the fact that it's a huge part of the dinner and that family members who are carnivorous do fight over two things: the drumsticks and wishbone.

To bring peace to the table, I suggested we save the wishbones, gold-leaf them, and keep them as souvenirs. It's a keepsake that somehow makes sense in my mind, and maybe for some of you it does, too. When you collect enough over several years, display them on a pretty platter or keepsake box. This project may sound crazy to some of you, but I promise the end result is gloriously gorgeous.

HOW TO: Begin with the wishbone and scrub off as much flesh, meat, grease, and gravy from it as possible using warm soapy water and a scrub brush at the sink. Pat it dry. ✪ Then insert the wishbone in a container full of hydrogen peroxide for a few days with the lid on; this will draw out impurities and disinfect it at the same time. Do not boil or bleach the bones, as this will just force whatever marrow or grease is inside the bone to stay embedded; it will smell in a few weeks if you do this.

With a dry and disinfected wishbone, use a gold-leafing pen to paint the outside. ✪ Tie a small hangtag on with the year, if desired, or stamp the bone with a mini alphabet kit to personalize it.

CHOPSTICK TRIVET

SUPPLIES: 10-INCH METAL HOSE CLAMP ⊕ FLATHEAD SCREWDRIVER ⊕ LOTS OF CHOPSTICKS (APPROXIMATELY 200 PAIRS).

This is another DUH upcycling project, and what I mean by that is this: You would have to be completely inept if you're unable to make this chopstick trivet. And I don't mean to insult the novice crafters; what I mean is that the steps to make this are so easy it can pretty much be instructed through Twitter: stick chopsticks in . . . twist . . . clamp. #upcyclingiseasy.

First, I'm breaking my upcycling rule a wee bit here by using new chopsticks. The reason is I bought 200 bamboo chopsticks for about $5 in New York's Chinatown a few years ago on a whim, and never used them. If you want to stay true to the upcycling roots, you can also use trimmed sticks or bamboo stalks from the yard; just be sure they are perfectly even and identical as possible in size. Or if you have a crazy stash of wooden pencils, it can also be used. The point is this: Anything that is about the height and shape of these chopsticks will also work, but buying new chopsticks is also okay, too.

HOW TO: Turn the hose clamp on its side (so it looks like a big "O" propped up) and fill it with the chopsticks. ⊕ When it's full and snug, *then* you can flip it up and finesse it so the chopsticks are all pin-straight and even. ⊕ Then use the flathead screwdriver to tighten it so it's nice and secure.

THE EASIEST LEAF COASTERS

SUPPLIES: OLD SWEATSHIRT ✚ CHALK ✚ SCISSORS.

With all of the coaster projects I've created over the years, one might think I'm a bit fanatical about protecting the wood surfaces in my home. It could not be further from the truth; in fact, I rarely use coasters in my own home and actually like the character my antique wood furniture gets from water rings and drops of stray red wine. But guests who come to Casa Seo don't like my casual nature and insist on a coaster. So, being forced to be hospitable, I came up with this project.

All you need is an old sweatshirt and some basic drawing skills. Cut open the sweatshirt so you have a square piece to work with. Draw some leaves with chalk and cut them out with scissors. Wipe the excess chalk off and then start pouring drinks.

When I lived in New York City, in a tiny one-bedroom apartment in the West Village—despite the small size of my home—I made do with the lack of space and threw dinner parties all the time. Once, when a friend called at the last minute and begged if they could bring a friend, the gracious host in me said, "Why not?" The paranoid, anal-retentive planner inside me totally freaked out about where to seat them.

And that is how this upcycling idea was born.

EXTRA BOOK SEATING

SUPPLIES: 2 EXTRA-LARGE BELTS ⊕ STACK OF BOOKS.

It really helps to have two extra-large men's belts. And I'm talking really, really large belts that could only be found in a specialty store like a Big and Tall shop. You can also search thrift stores to find them since you only need two. Then it's a matter of stacking books, wrapping the belts around them, and tightening them up.

There is something so adorable about these turkey place markers that I don't think they should be relegated to the kid's table. But whether you use them for children or grown-ups, I do think it would be a nice project to involve the kids in making.

I used new crayons in the turkeys pictured here, but you can also make do with used crayons. Just sharpen them up so they come to a point to mimic the colorful feathers found on the real deal.

TURKEY PLACE MARKERS

SUPPLIES: RED POTATOES ✪ TOOTHPICKS ✪ CORDLESS DRILL BIT (OPTIONAL) ✪ CRAYONS ✪ PARING KNIFE ✪ PAINT CHIPS.

HOW TO: Pick a medium-sized red potato for the body and a small round one for the head; use a toothpick to attach them together. ✪ Snap some toothpicks in half and stick them into the base of the larger potato to make the feet. ✪ Jab crayons in the back (you can use a cordless drill bit to get the holes started, if needed), and insert a crayon tip into the smaller potato to make the beak by simply jabbing it into the potato. ✪ Run a paring knife across the back, insert a paint chip, and write the guest's name.

FLOATING JAR-LID CANDLES

SUPPLIES: METAL JAR LIDS ⊕ 1-INCH CANDLEWICKS ⊕ OLD CANDLE ⊕ SMALL AND LARGE SAUCE PANS.

The next time somebody asks "Can I help?" when you're in the kitchen prepping your Turkey Day feast, don't be courteous and send them off with a fresh glass of wine to mind the fire. Instead, delegate this project to them. These floating candles are such a cinch to make, your guests can make them as you cook away, and still have time to keep their Thanksgiving Day buzz going.

I don't know why, but certain jar lids float in water and some sink. So you'll need to save a collection of metal jar lids (don't use plastic since it can be a fire hazard) and toss them into a sink full of water. Save the ones that float. You can use these floating candles as a centerpiece for the table or anywhere you want a little ambience.

HOW TO: Over a double boiler, melt an old candle in a smaller sauce pan that's inside a larger sauce pan that's simmering about an inch of water. ⊕ Stir until melted. ⊕ Place a pre-tabbed 1-inch candlewick inside the jar lid; one will do, but you can add a second wick if it's an extra-large lid. ⊕ Pour the melted wax inside each lid. ⊕ Allow to cool before using.

UPCYCLED CIGAR-BOX TEA GIFT

SUPPLIES: CIGAR BOX ◆ SELECTION OF TEAS AND CONDIMENTS.

I hate to admit something as vile as smoking inspired this project, but it did. I just love the wooden cigar boxes you'll often see stacked up outside cigar stores, with a little sign saying they're for sale for just a few dollars apiece. I'm glad the owners of those shops appreciated the handsome nature of these boxes and didn't just toss them into the trash. I just wish their original purpose was something a bit healthier.

The idea for this gift is pretty straightforward: People like drinking tea and when there's a variety to choose from, it helps keep the peace between those who adore green tea and those who only sip soothing chamomile. But what I like best is that this is the sort of hostess gift that is truly useful and can be cracked open at the end of a meal.

HOW TO: It's easy—just put whatever you think should go in the box: I like individual organic tea bags, a bottle of honey, and some decorative tea spoons if you want to splurge.
◆ Fit them into the cigar box, close it up, and tie it all together with a pretty ribbon.

Yes, I know, there is nothing wrong with burning regular white pillar candles. But for you die-hard upcyclers out there, you may sympathize with me that if you have the ability to transform them into something way nicer, why wouldn't you? Besides, it's not like I can give someone a set of white generic candles as a gift; when they've adorned with whisper-soft feathers, leaves, and shells, it's just a far better gift.

WAXY NATURE CANDLES

SUPPLIES: WHILE PILLAR CANDLES (THESE ARE FROM HOMEGOODS) ⊕ HAMMER ⊕ TOWEL ⊕ SMALL AND LARGE SAUCEPANS (DOUBLE BOILER) ⊕ FOAM BRUSH ⊕ FOUND OBJECTS FROM OUTDOORS ⊕ OLD WHITE CANDLE.

HOW TO: You need to either find a white candle that no longer burns or sacrifice one for this project (I prefer the former, but do whatever is convenient for you). Smash that candle into lots of smaller pieces using a hammer; wrap the candle in a towel and smash away to keep the mess to a minimum. ⊕ Melt that white candle over a double boiler until melted. ⊕ Dip a foam brush in the melted wax and coat the back of a leaf, feather, or shell and use it like glue to attach it to the front of a pillar candle. ⊕ Then dip the whole thing several times until it's coated and frosted.

Cupcakes are one of the sweet treats that really can be enjoyed and appreciated any time of the year. Fall cupcakes can take on a seasonal flair—think pumpkin or candy-corn flavors—and are a new twist on the traditional Thanksgiving Day dessert offerings. One way to bring your sweetly made treats to the party in a handy carry-all is to save the cardboard containers you use to carry your morning run of lattes and cappuccinos for the office.

COFFEE CARRYOUT
CUPCAKE-CARRYING CASE

SUPPLIES: 2 CARDBOARD COFFEE CONTAINERS ✛ RIBBON.

HOW TO: Just fill the four compartments with cupcakes (think miniatures, not extra-large treats!) and add a matching container on top to keep them snug and separate; tie a ribbon around the whole thing to keep it secure, and carry.

BLEACHED DENIM NAPKINS

SUPPLIES: OLD DENIM JEANS ✪ PINKING SHEARS ✪ FABRIC NAPKIN (TEMPLATE) ✪ IRON ✪ BLEACH PEN.

If you've ever eaten a messy batch of cheese fries or buffalo wings with a ten-year-old boy (in my case, my nephew), you know that they also think their blue jeans are also interchangeable as wearable napkins. It was at a birthday party at an unnamed chain restaurant, where I watched him eat greasy finger food and clean his hands right on the front of his jeans, that I got the inspiration for this upcycled denim-napkin project.

The best jeans to use are the ones that you already have. But a visit to your local Goodwill store will reveal a treasure trove of possibilities. I like getting the maximum fabric for my buck, so I head to the men's section and look for plus-sized jeans, almost big enough for my whole self to stand in one leg. That size of jeans (I paid $5) is just enough to create a stack of napkins.

HOW TO: Launder the jeans in hot water with detergent and tumble dry. ✪ Cut each leg off using pinking shears and then cut along the seam of the leg to make a flat piece of fabric; repeat with the other leg. ✪ Use an existing fabric napkin that you like the size of as your template and place on top of the denim fabric; cut out the napkins. Iron your napkins and use the fine-tip side of the bleach pen to draw whatever pattern you want. ✪ Write initials, use a stencil to make a design, or go freehand and do polka dots.

Allow the bleach markings to dry overnight so they can fully saturate the denim fabric and turn the marked sections white. ✪ Rinse under cold water and dry in the dryer.

Think of the Disney classic *Lady and the Tramp*. The iconic scene where they share a plate of spaghetti and meatballs at an Italian restaurant with a red-and-white checkered table-cloth, illuminated by a single candle in an upcycled Chianti bottle. Sweet. Romantic. Darling.

For your Thanksgiving table, might I suggest these lovely wineglass tea-light holders to illuminate? They add a certain glow and ambience and you just might have all the materials you need to make these upcycled lights.

WINEGLASS TEA-LIGHT HOLDERS

SUPPLIES: WINEGLASSES ✪ LED FLAMELESS TEA-LIGHT CANDLES ✪ PAPER CHANDELIER LAMP SHADES.

HOW TO: Start off with wineglasses—chipped or perfectly good—and insert an LED light on the inside. Why LED? They are flameless and safe, so don't even think about swapping in a real tea-light candle. ✪ Then place a chandelier-style lampshade on top.

Come Thanksgiving time, the leftover mini pumpkins and gourds you have piled up by the front door can be a sad state of affairs. They can be mushy, dried-up, or have stems that are falling off like dead limbs on a tree. While the greenest thing to do is to toss them all into the compost bin, I thought the dried-up stems would be adorable to use for these faux upcycled gourds for the Thanksgiving table.

FALL GOURD PLACE MARKER HOLDERS

SUPPLIES: YARN OR THICK STRING ✪ DRIED PUMPKIN STEMS ✪ HOT-GLUE GUN AND GLUE STICKS ✪ OFFICE-SUPPLY STORE MANILA TAGS ✪ ALPHABET STAMP SET AND INKPAD (OPTIONAL).

HOW TO: Start by choosing a colorful yarn or string (think autumnal colors) and wrap it around and around on itself until you get a plump little pumpkin. ✪ Using the hot-glue gun, adhere a dried stem to the top. ✪ Write the guest's name on a small manila tag and tie it to the stem.

THANKSGIVING DAY MENUS

SUPPLIES: LARGE FLAT METAL TRAY ⊕ SANDPAPER ⊕ CHALKBOARD PAINT ⊕ SMALL FOAM BRUSH ⊕ CHALK.

What's for dinner? Of all the days of the year, that question has the most importance probably on Thanksgiving Day. Instead of rattling off each dish like a waiter at a five-star restaurant ("the casserole has thinly sliced potatoes roasted in a creamy Bechamel sauce . . . "), let them read the menu with this adorable upcycled chalkboard tray.

After the Thanksgiving holiday, don't stash it away for next year's feast: mount it in the kitchen and use it as a memo or reminder board the rest of the year.

HOW TO: Look for the perfect tray. I find that flea markets and thrift stores are the best places to get silverplated trays for just a few dollars. Leave the valuable antiques for the serious collectors and hunt for a large, flat tray. If it's tarnished or marred, don't worry: you're going to paint it anyway and a little tarnish adds character along the edges.

Scratch the surface with sandpaper; it will help the paint stick better. ⊕ Paint a thin coat of chalkboard paint all over the surface. You can tape off the sections you don't want painted or just carefully do it freehand using a small foam brush. ⊕ Allow to dry for 45 minutes. ⊕ Repeat. ⊕ And add one more coat if needed.

Allow to dry overnight. ⊕ Rub the whole surface with chalk to help "set" the chalkboard paint and wipe off and then write whatever you want on top.

BONUS PROJECT: See the adorable corn napkin holders in the photo? It's a cinch to make: Just take a toilet paper cardboard tube, wrap it in bubble wrap (using glue to attach it to the bubble wrap), and cover it with yellow spray paint.

THANKSGIVING
•ROASTED TURKEY
•MASHED POTATOES
•STUFFING
•PUMPKIN PIE

CHAPTER NINE:
CHRISTMAS AND HANUKKAH

Christmas used to be a big deal for me, in July.

As a former magazine editor, I had to think about issues months ahead of time, when we'd plan our December–January issues in the middle of a heat wave. Ideas had to be formulated, approved, produced, photographed, and laid out before they'd go to press and be on newsstands in early November.

So there I would be at my home (which somehow always ended up being the location for these shoots) hanging wreaths, stringing lights, and wrapping empty boxes tied up with string to lay under a beautifully decorated Christmas tree. This would ultimately be met with stares and confusion by the neighbors who I would eventually need to explain: No, I have not lost my mind.

Christmas and Hanukkah was a big deal at our magazines because these two holidays are important to all of our readers. They mark significant religious celebrations, but also represent a time of rest and celebration at the end of what was surely a busy and eventful year. And if there's one holiday we tend to invest the most time, money, and energy into, it's definitely what happens in the month of December.

This chapter is a best-of-the-best of ideas from my years as a decorating editor. A few have been featured in the pages of *Country Home* or *Better Homes & Gardens,* but the majority are my favorite ideas that somehow didn't make the pages of the magazines. I suspected there was a reason why they didn't make the cut, and now I know: to be in this book!

PLASTIC SHOPPING-BAG HOLIDAY ORNAMENTS

SUPPLIES: PLASTIC SHOPPING BAGS IN ALL SORTS OF COLORS + SCISSORS.

One of the joys of this upcycling project is how easy it is to make. There's no glue, no weird knitting tricks, and no scarcity of supplies. The challenge here (unless you want an all-white-ball tree) is finding a variety of colorful plastic bags. This is the hard part: be your eco-self and ask your friends and family if you can raid their used-bag drawer to find bags. Don't overconsume (or, horrors, ask for multiple bags) when you shop; it just isn't the most ecological thing to do.

HOW TO: Lay a plastic bag flat and cut it into strips approximately 2 inches thick; make about four strips total. + Tie each strip to each other by knotting them together. Roll it up into a ball and leave about 5 inches to make a loop at the end of the ball. + To make larger plastic shopping-bag ornaments, start with more strips before rolling it up by simply using more bags.

BONUS PROJECT: Save those Styrofoam packing peanuts for a festive garland. Just thread a needle with string and string 'em up like popcorn; decorate away on your evergreen tree.

BONUS DECORATING TIP: Save some bubble wrap and use it to wrap around the base of the evergreen tree for a modern, frosty decorative touch.

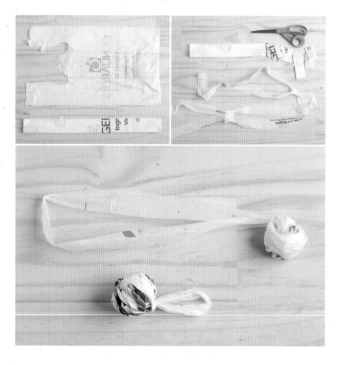

If there is ever an Olympic event on upcycling Altoid mint tins, I'd walk away with the gold medal, hands down. It's not because I'm the craftiest or most creative person in the world, I am simply the most obsessed. Ever since I first saw the tins of fresh-breath candies, I've been drawn to the iconic, durable package. I simply have not been able to ever just toss an empty tin into the recycling bin.

So, whether they get made into mini first-aid kits or hangover kits for New Year's, it always starts with an Altoid tin.

ALTOID-TIN
GIFT CARD TINS

SUPPLIES: ALTOID MINT TINS ✪ DECORATIVE PAPER ✪ X-ACTO KNIFE ✪ WHITE CRAFT GLUE ✪ BRUSH ✪ GLITTER ✪ RIBBON.

HOW TO: You don't have to cover the outside of the tin with decorative paper, but if you don't, you are simply reusing an Altoid tin and not upcycling it. If aesthetics matter to you, it's easy to do: Spread craft glue on the top of the Altoid tin and lay it flat on a piece of pretty paper. ✪ Press it firmly in place and then use an X-Acto knife to trim off the excess along the edges for a clean finish. ✪ Do the same along the edges of the tin. ✪ Paint a thin layer of glue around the edges and sprinkle with glitter, place a gift card inside, and tie it all up with a ribbon.

STACKABLE COOKIE GIFT TINS

SUPPLIES: METAL COOKIE TINS ✛ ENAMEL PAINT ✛ SANDPAPER.

I don't know why, but when my friends and colleagues are Christmas shopping for me, the words "butter Danish cookies" must collectively come to mind to a lot of them. Why? Because that seems to be the go-to gift for me, come December. So for two weeks, stacks of these cookie tins live in my kitchen pantry as I get re-introduced to the glorious world of buttery, sugar-coated complex carbohydrates.

However these metal cookie tins come in your possession, you can upcycle them into useful storage tins in a few simple steps. I find they are great for storing office supplies, tea bags, or—if I ever tap into my inner Jamie Oliver—for holding homemade butter Danish cookies.

HOW TO: Take a piece of coarse sandpaper and rub it profusely all over the outside of the tin, scratching it up and removing as much of the printed material as possible. ✛ Wipe it clean with a damp rag. ✛ Paint several coats of enamel paint on the outside of the tin and allow to dry completely. To "age" them, randomly rub the dry paint with sandpaper, as desired.

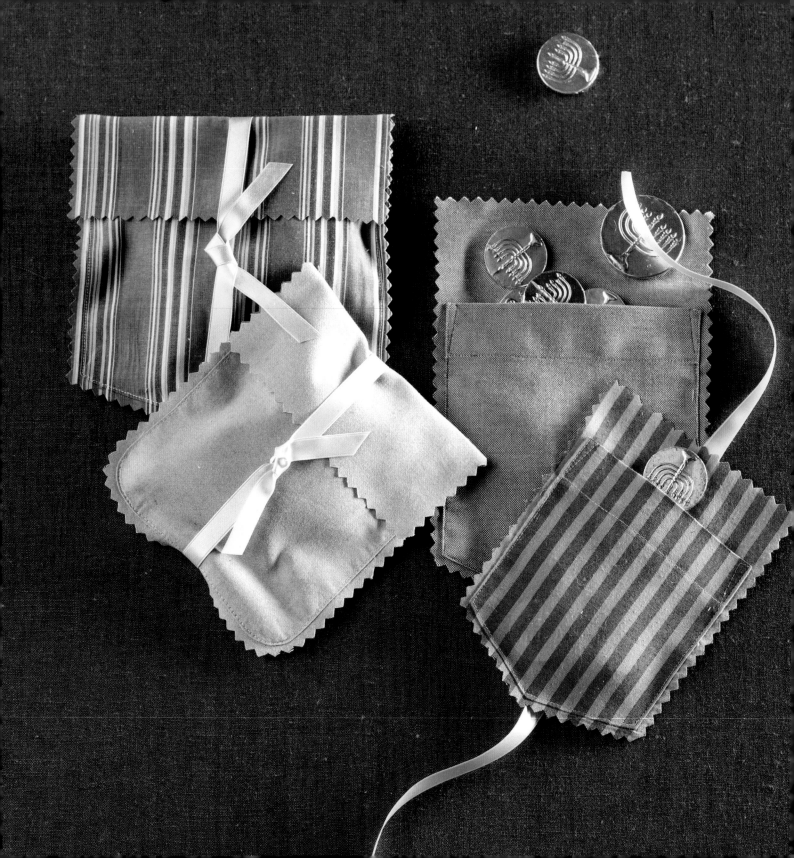

This is a lovely and easy upcycling idea to celebrate the giving of chocolate gelt coins during the festival of Hanukkah. If you don't have a stash of old men's dress shirts to use, a local thrift store is always a great place to find good shirts.

MEN'S SHIRT GELT BAGS

SUPPLIES: MEN'S DRESS SHIRTS ⊕ REGULAR SCISSORS ⊕ PINKING SHEARS ⊕ CHOCOLATE GELT COINS ⊕ RIBBON.

HOW TO: I find that using a pair of regular scissors to cut out the front section of the shirt where the pocket is makes the pinking part much easier. Use the pinking shears to cut around the sides and bottom of the pocket, all while keeping it intact as a pocket. ⊕ Cut approximately 1 to 2 inches above the pocket so you have a flap that can fold over to keep the gelt coins in place. ⊕ Fill the pocket with the chocolates, and tie the whole thing up secure with a piece of ribbon.

CRYSTALLIZED TENNIS BALLS

SUPPLIES: OLD TENNIS BALLS ✛ PLASTIC CONTAINER ✛ HOT WATER ✛ TABLESPOON ✛ BORAX DETERGENT ✛ EYE SCREW ✛ CHOPSTICK OR TWIG ✛ FLORIST WIRE.

If you've read this book from start to finish, you may recall that in the Spring chapter there was a project to crystallize silk flowers using Borax detergent (page 92). Let me stop you right here: This is the exact same project, but with completely different results.

So if you don't want to be bored with the tutorial instructions, just re-read the previous project and swap "flowers" to "tennis ball" and you'll be good to go.

But the reason I included it as a holiday project is that there was something so chillingly wintery about these finished crystallized balls that I couldn't include it in the spring-themed part of the book. The idea here is two-fold: If you have lots of tennis balls, you can make ornaments to hang from the tree. If you have just a few, these are just as pretty hung in a window as a suncatcher. Whatever reason, now we have one more idea beyond playing fetch with the dog for making use of old tennis balls.

HOW TO: Twist a small eye screw into the tennis ball. ✛ Twist some florist wire around the eye screw and then around a chopstick or twig; place it inside the plastic container so the ball hangs inside without touching the sides or bottom. ✛ Remove the tennis ball and fill the container with hot water and eight tablespoons of Borax; stir until clear. ✛ Submerge the ball and let it sit undisturbed overnight or for 24 hours.

BONUS PROJECT: One alternative is to simply pin beads all over a tennis ball. Thread a pin with a small glass bead (small enough so it doesn't thread through the head of the pin) and add a larger bead and poke it into the tennis ball. Repeat until covered.

There are two seasonal holiday items that put my eco-rage on overdrive: One is plastic Easter grass and the other are bags of artificial decorative snow. Both are petroleum-based, impossible to recycle, and just end up being tossed into the landfill to sit and never decompose.

I showed you how to take scrap paper and make your own fake Easter grass, and now I'm going to share my fake-snow tip: Just toss chunks of old Styrofoam into a blender. Save Styrofoam whenever something fragile is shipped to you, cut it down to small chunks, turn on the blender, and toss it in and watch it be decimated into fine, fluffy, fake snow.

UPCYCLED CONTAINER "SNOW" GLOBES

SUPPLIES: VARIETY OF KITCHEN GLASS CONTAINERS WITH LIDS ◆ E-6000 GLUE ◆ STYROFOAM ◆ BLENDER ◆ PLASTIC TOYS AND TREES.

Since we're on this fake-spree, why not make fake-snow globes? Raid your kitchen for unused glass containers—jam jars, sugar shakers, syrup pourers, salt shakers—and fill them with charming plastic animals and artificial mini trees; I found these on a trip to my local Michaels store. Glue them to the bottom using E-6000 glue by holding the figurines by the top and securing them inside; sprinkle lots of homemade artificial snow inside, screw on the lid, and you're done.

OFFICE-SUPPLY GINGERBREAD HOUSE

SUPPLIES: TWO CARDBOARD BOXES ✪ OFFICE-SUPPLY STICKERS ✪ POST-IT NOTES ✪ X-ACTO KNIFE ✪ LED STRING LIGHTS.

When I was a child, I begged my parents to let me make a gingerbread house. There was something fascinating about the idea of a three-dimensional home that was totally edible with crisp gingerbread, sweet frosting, and candy. So they let me make one with a more kid-friendly approach of graham crackers, store-bought frosting, and whatever candy was around the house.

I left my homemade creation on a platter under the Christmas tree that night and—like any reality-check moment—woke up to find a mouse gnawing away at it in the morning. I vowed, ever since that horrific day, to never make an edible gingerbread house again.

That sad story is the inspiration for this project, but I think the idea is perfectly adorable, non-perishable, and—this is the best part—reusable. Make it once and bring it out every Christmas season.

HOW TO: Start with a sturdy cardboard box for the base of the house. ✪ Use an X-Acto knife to cut down the top on an angle so it forms the shape of a house. ✪ Fashion a strip of cardboard to be the roof of the house and set it aside. ✪ Use the same X-Acto knife to cut out windows and a door, all over the house. ✪ Decorate the outside using office-supply stickers and "shingle" the roof with Post-it notes. ✪ Attach the roof and fill the inside with LED string lights to illuminate it.

Cardboard is a hugely underrated upcycling material. Sure, it's not as luxurious as an old cashmere sweater you can upcycle into a luxurious throw pillow, but it's a raw material in its purest form that can be reimagined into a million different new things.

This is an upcycling project that I know will become one of my holiday perennial favorites. The reason? It's so simple to do and the ornaments are just gosh-darn cute. Yes, I get mushy during the holidays.

CARDBOARD "GINGERBREAD" ORNAMENTS

SUPPLIES: CORRUGATED CARDBOARD ✪ SCISSORS ✪ HOLE PUNCH ✪ WHITE PUFFY SHIRT PAINT ✪ RIBBON.

HOW TO: Cut out silhouettes—a star, a gingerbread man, a deer—from an old cardboard box. ✪ Squeeze puffy shirt paint along the edges as if it's frosting; allow to dry completely. ✪ Make a hole using a hole punch, and run a skinny piece of ribbon through it and hang on a tree.

HOT-AIR BALLOON LIGHTBULB ORNAMENTS

SUPPLIES: BURNT-OUT LIGHTBULB ○ **CHAMPAGNE-CORK CAGE** ○ **MOD PODGE GLUE** ○ **TISSUE PAPER** ○ **SCISSORS** ○ **STRING.**

This project may be on the endangered-crafting list if CFL and super-high LED lightbulbs become the way of the future. But as long as people continue to use old-fashioned incandescent lightbulbs, that just means there are going to be burnt-out bulbs for me to upcycle. So, check for dead bulbs from your home and get crafting with this project.

I'm not sure what screams holiday about hot-air balloon ornaments, but they are the right size to hang from a tree and the ball-ish shape of the top of the balloon does look like a traditional ball ornament. So, if you can look beyond the spring nature of the design, I think a collection of these will look rather dashing on your tree. And here's a tip for those of you who don't indulge in champers on a regular basis: You can ask your local restaurant, wine store, or anywhere where they serve champagne to save you the metal cages that secure the champagne corks in place. These are always tossed and are easy to save, especially if you ask really, really nicely.

HOW TO: Cut tissue paper into small strips that will cover the outside of the bulb, from the base of the socket to the top of the bulb. ○ Cover the whole bulb in Mod Podge glue and attach the tissue paper on top. ○ Wait for it to dry slightly (about 10 minutes; do other bulbs as you wait) and then apply a thin layer of more Mod Podge on top to seal it in. ○ To get the cool striped appearance, use strips of identical tissue paper and attach them one at a time, alternating colors. ○ Allow to dry completely. ○ Tie two pieces of string around the socket tightly, and bring them up along the side of the bulb and knot at top. ○ Leave excess so you have enough string to loop around the tree to hang it. ○ Twist a champagne cork cage around the bottom to make the "basket" for the balloon.

UPCYCLED DREIDEL

SUPPLIES: JAR LID ✪ ACORN NUT ✪ BOLT ✪ REGULAR NUT ✪ CORDLESS DRILL WITH LARGE DRILL BIT.

Okay, let me start by saying I understand a traditional dreidel has four sides engraved with four different Hebrew letters, and it's spun with the understanding that you bet on which letter ends up showing when the dreidel stops spinning.

But traditions change and for this upcycling project, we used some creative freedom from the traditional design for something a bit more modern. And after showing it to my Jewish friends, they agreed it was a fun interpretation and should be in the book.

The thing about this upcycled dreidel is that it spins like you wouldn't believe. My photo-shoot team who shot this book constantly played with them to the point that I had to take them and hide them so work could be done. If grown adults can't get enough of these, I'm sure kids will adore them, too.

HOW TO: Use the cordless drill to make a hole in the middle of the jar lid. ✪ Thread the regular nut onto the bolt, leaving enough space for the end of the bolt to just stick through the jar lid. ✪ Then thread the acorn nut on tight against the bottom of the jar lid. ✪ Spin away!

HAPPY-HOLIDAYS BANNER SIGN

SUPPLIES: DRIED-UP PENS AND MARKERS ✪ BROKEN PENCILS ✪ HOT-GLUE GUN AND GLUE STICKS ✪ YARN OR STRING ✪ HOLE PUNCH ✪ SCISSORS ✪ OFFICE-SUPPLY PAPER.

A few years ago, I was working as a consultant for the eco-friendly cleaning-supply company Method. We were doing a photo shoot in their office, showcasing some green ideas for entertaining, and after looking at the digital photos on the computer screen, I felt something was missing from the wall. Was it a piece of art? Did it need color from paint? And it occurred to me that it just needed a punch of fun from a garland.

Tapping into my inner MacGyver, I raided the office for whatever people were willing to spare with and—this is not a shocker—it was useless junk from inside their desk drawers. But it was that stash of trash that inspired what I think is a perfect example of the art of upcycling.

By the way, you can do this project with almost any message you want, so think "Happy Birthday," Way to Go Dad (or Mom!)" and "Happy New Year's."

HOW TO: Cut thick office-supply paper (think cardstock) into circles. ✪ With a hot-glue gun, attach dried-up pens, markers, and broken pencils to the front of each circle to spell out a letter. ✪ Repeat until your phrase is completed. ✪ Use a hole punch to make two holes at the top of each circle, and run yarn or string through it to make the garland.

I call this my Studio-Apartment or Office-Cubicle Christmas tree. Why? Because it's small, doesn't need water, and I think is actually more creatively impressive than a ten-foot-tall White House Christmas tree.

Who doesn't love the iconic Charlie Brown Christmas special where the sad, wimpy, loser tree becomes the hero evergreen at the end? You can celebrate that by making your own—and all without having to actually cut down a tree!

CHARLIE BROWN TREE

SUPPLIES: 2 WOODEN PAINT STIRRERS ⊕ SMALL WOOD SCREW ⊕ PINE BRANCH ⊕ ALUMINUM FOIL ⊕ SCISSORS ⊕ HOLE PUNCH ⊕ TWINE.

HOW TO: Attach a flimsy pine branch to two wooden paint stirrers with a wood screw; crossing the paint stirrers into an "X" and twisting the screw from the bottom up into the branch should do the trick. ⊕ Take some old (but clean) aluminum foil and fold it into several layers. ⊕ Use sharp scissors to cut out a star from the folded foil. ⊕ Punch a hole, and hang with twine from the end of the tree.

UGLY SWEATER FABRIC-COVERED WREATH

SUPPLIES: TACKY SWEATERS ✪ HARD STYROFOAM WREATH FRAMES (FROM MICHAELS CRAFT STORES) ✪ STRAIGHT SEWING PINS ✪ SEQUINS, POM-POMS, AND BEADS ✪ SCISSORS ✪ WOODEN CRAFT SILHOUETTE (OPTIONAL).

I've never gotten a seasonal sweater as a gift, but I've heard horror stories. Just think of the movie *Bridget Jones Diary,* the scene where Renée Zellweger runs into Colin Firth at a Christmas party and he's wearing that super tacky sweater his parents gifted to him. If you've got a stash of sparkly, festive sweaters you just can't bear to wear, you can still bring them out of the closet for the holidays by upcycling them into these cozy fabric-covered wreaths.

By the way, if you are lucky enough to not be the recipient of a glow-in-the-dark Rudolph the Red-Nosed Reindeer sweater, you can always raid the local Salvation Army or Goodwill store for some tacky picks. My advice: Find ones that are encrusted with rhinestones and beads. Yes, you'll get a stare at checkout, but they'll look impressive as a wreath.

HOW TO: Use scissors to cut the sweaters into fabric strips that can wrap around the Styrofoam wreath frame. ✪ Wrap a sweater piece and pin it right into the wreath. ✪ Continue until the whole wreath is covered with patches of different sweaters. ✪ Embellish it with sequins, pom-poms, and beads by pinning those also onto the wreath. ✪ You can also add a wooden craft-store silhouette (I chose a moose here, to play up the wintery theme) if desired.

UPCYCLED MENORAH

SUPPLIES: GLASS BOTTLES ✛ PLASTIC FUNNEL ✛ LATEX PAINT ✛ WHITE PILLAR CANDLES.

Here's how this project came about: I had a giant collection of old glass bottles all over the house. Using a plastic funnel, I poured paint inside the bottles, swirled it around so it coated the inside of the bottle, completely poured out the excess, and let it dry. Then I took a small collection of white pillar candles and found the ones that could snugly hold the candles. Instant menorah!

I love the month of December, but even when the festivities are over and you're planning your New Year's Eve bash, it's time to think a little bit about storing it all up so you can celebrate all over again next year.

AND WHEN IT'S TIME TO PACK IT UP . . .

In the summer months, when tomatoes and peaches are abundant, supermarkets are often overrun with cardboard shipping boxes with plastic inserts, designed to keep their precious produce from banging into each other. You'll see piles of these boxes tossed into the trash compactor out back, and eventually either sent to the recycling facility or landfill.

If you ask nicely, they will give you these boxes for free. And what I've found is that they are the perfect size to hold all of your delicate glass Christmas ornament balls perfectly. Snug, intact, safe, and each slim box is stackable.

So that phrase "Christmas in July"? Start thinking produce boxes, and you'll be prepared come December 26.

ACKNOWLEDGMENTS

It is one thing to sit in a room with your book editor and say "Wouldn't an upcycling-entertaining book be a great follow-up to *Upcycling?*" and another entirely to actually conceive, produce, shoot, and write it. But with all the blood (paper cuts), sweat (hauling large trees to the set), and tears (mostly allergies, some real), the people behind this book are really what took it from a bright idea in my head to reality.

First, I have to thank the team at Running Press for believing in my upcycling concept so much. I have an incredible book editor, Jennifer Kasius, who not only lets me run off and create the book I always envisioned, but can be a true, trusted confidante (trust me, I have tried but failed to get dirt on all those *Real Housewives* she does books with . . . and I *can be* persistent). Jason Kayser, for the fantastic cover and interior design, and Craig Herman, for making sure my books get onto a national platform known as the talk-show circuit, when each book comes out.

I owe a huge debt of gratitude to the many talk-show hosts who share their incredible platforms to let me show millions of people how to upcycle: Kathie Lee Gifford and Hoda Kotb, Nate Berkus, Anderson Cooper, Rachael Ray, Wendy Williams, Billy Bush and Kit Hoover, and all the hosts in local markets who patiently watch me talk about the virtues of saving a garbage bag full of wine corks to upcycle into a myriad of household objects. And many thanks to Katie Lee, Johnny Iuzzini, and Deborah Needleman for their kind words of support for this book.

The folks who help me with our company: my literary agent Joy Tutela, my business-minded managers Tom Carr and Steven Pregiato, the best talent agent I could ever ask for, Maggie Dumais with Mary Douris, and all the designers who interpret my vision for our line of home products into the gorgeous pieces they are today. And to my friends at Michaels craft stores, Lowe's Home Improvement, T.J. Maxx, Marshalls, and HomeGoods, I cannot say thank you enough for all the support.

I am so lucky to have had an incredible team of support when creating this book: the beautiful photography skills of Laura Moss, the styling extraordinaire Sarah Cave along with assistant stylist Eddie Gee and Peter Dolkas, and none of these photos would exist if someone didn't wear the tech-geek hat, so much thanks to Leonard Mazzone.

But most importantly, I want to thank all the readers who have embraced the upcycling concept. I want to thank you for sending me tweets, sharing your own upcycling projects, and even for commenting how to improve on many of my own ideas. Without you, there would be no book, and I would be a total fool if I didn't thank you most importantly for being there.

—Danny Seo

INDEX

57

58

62

65

66

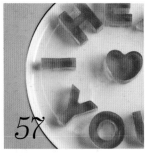

69

70

72

75

76

79

80

84

87

88

91

92

95

96

99

100

103

104

107

110

113

114

117

118

120

123

124

127

128

131

132

135

136

139

142

145

146

149

150

153

154

154

154

157

158

161

162

165

166

169

172

175

176

179

180

183

184

187

188

191

192

195

196

199

200

204

207

208

211

212